P9-CAN-225

Parties and Their Environments

Parties and Their Environments

Limits to Reform?

Robert Harmel
Texas A & M University

Kenneth Janda
Northwestern University

Longman

New York & London

PARTIES AND THEIR ENVIRONMENTS
Limits to Reform?

Longman Inc., 19 West 44th Street, New York, N.Y. 10036
Associated companies, branches, and representatives
throughout the world.

Copyright © 1982 by Longman Inc.

All rights reserved. No part of this publication may be
reproduced, stored in a retrieval system, or transmitted
in any form or by any means, electronic, mechanical,
photocopying, recording, or otherwise, without the prior
permission of the publisher.

Developmental Editor: Irving R. Rockwood
Editorial and Design Supervisor: Frances Althaus
Manufacturing and Production Supervisor: Robin B. Besofsky

Library of Congress Cataloging in Publication Data
Harmel, Robert, 1950-
  Parties and their environments.

  Bibliography: p.
  Includes index.
  1. Political parties — United States. 2. Democratic .
Party (U.S.) 3. Republican Party (U.S.) I. Janda,
Kenneth. II. Title.
JK2261.H27   324.273   81–8357
ISBN 0-582-28299-3   AACR2
ISBN 0-582-28298-5 (pbk.)

Manufactured in the United States of America
9 8 7 6 5 4 3 2 1

To Bob's parents,
    Clarence and Clara Harmel
and to Ken's daughters,
    Susan and Katy Janda

Contents

Preface

This book is about the place of political parties in democratic government and about proposals for changing the American parties to make them perform their role more satisfactorily. It is not our primary purpose in this book simply to chronicle those proposals and attempts to accomplish them, however. Our purpose is to address a question that arises out of the American experience with party reform: To what extent are the parties free to change themselves, given constraints placed on them by their physical, socioeconomic, and political/governmental environments? In other words, to what extent are parties shaped by the settings within which they operate and thereby externally limited in their attempts to reform?

Our answers will be suggested by systematic comparisons of a large sample of competitive parties in democratic systems worldwide. In Chapters 3 through 6, we explore the effects of various environmental factors, as well as the environment generally, on four important dimensions of party character: ideology, degree of organization, centralization of power, and cohesion in the legislature. Then, in the last two chapters, we bring the comparative findings to bear on the American situation. Critical to that discussion is the notion of a changing American environment, with changing parameters for party reform.

We owe a debt of gratitude to a number of individuals and organizations who helped with this project in one way or another. Sam Kirkpatrick and Ted Gurr, in their respective capacities as head of the Department of Political Science at Texas A&M and chairman of the department at Northwestern, were extremely helpful in providing good counsel and services during the course of the study. Texas A&M's Liberal Arts Council made funding available in 1978, which allowed us to work together in Evanston during the critical, initial phase of this project. The cross-national parties data used for analyses in Chapters 3 through 6 were originally collected at Northwestern University with Kenneth Janda as principal investigator, with major funding provided by National Science Foundation user grants GS-1418, GS-2523, and GS-27081. Janda was also supported during the winter of 1973 by the American Enterprise Institute. We gratefully acknowledge those sources of support.

We also thank George Edwards, Steve Chan, and Harvey Tucker for their sage advice; Keith Hamm, Edward Portis, John Robertson, and Robert Thompson for reading and commenting on various parts of the manuscript; Jim Dyer, Michael Ward, Alexander Hicks, and Michael Gant for help with some methodological problems; Carl Richard, Brian Boudreaux, and Paula Maples for their invaluable help as graduate assistants; and Edna Lumpkin, Lucille Mayer, and Kathy Jones for their exceptional secretarial assistance. We would also like to express our thanks to our developmental editor, Irving Rockwood, whose early and continued interest in the project helped to keep us going.

Finally, we want to thank each other. To paraphrase a well-known quote: Coauthors never die; they just keep coming back to point out each other's errors. For that large and critical service, each of us is especially grateful to the other.

Robert Harmel
Kenneth Janda

June 1981

Parties and Their Environments

1

Parties in Democracy and Party Reform in America

Almost as old as the history of political parties is the history of attempts to change them, to make them "better." Models have even been developed by which to judge a party's organization, goals, and ultimate success, and toward which parties presumably should be changed. The story of party reform in the United States alone consumes a large and interesting literature. This book, too, deals with the topic of party reform. But, unlike other books on the subject, this one does not focus on the *politics* of party reform but on the *possibility* of party reform. It asks how much parties can be changed given the nature of their political and social environment, which may impose important limits on party reform. We ask the question with reference not only to the American parties, but to all competitive parties in democratic systems. We begin by considering the role of parties in modern government.

THE PREVALENCE OF PARTIES

Today it is difficult to imagine national politics without political parties. Yet such was the case until early in the nineteenth century, when the first of the modern political parties was formed in the United States. Britain, often used as the "model" for Western party systems, did not have a modern political party until 1867, when a major extension of the suffrage created a need for parties to educate and to organize the mass of new voters.[1]

Although political parties are a relatively youthful invention among modern political institutions, they have multiplied rapidly and have come to play an important role in organizing the politics of most political systems today. There are now hundreds of parties in the world, and they are found in all but a handful of countries and in all types of polities. While even autocratic regimes have come to value their own brand of restrictive party, it is in modern democratic systems that the greatest importance is attributed to the contributions of political parties to politics.

In fact, the literature abounds with statements that political parties are *necessary* for democratic government. While some authors hedge their evaluations,[2] others speak unequivocally about the relationship. Schattschneider flatly maintains that "political parties created democracy and that modern democracy is unthinkable save in terms of the parties." Scarcely less sweeping are Pennock's assertion that "democracies universally are characterized by the institution of political parties" and Merkl's that "popular government in all its distinctive patterns has seemed to require parties to mobilize the people and to articulate their needs." With comparable bluntness Casselini states, "Every democratic state has at least two political parties, and its party system—the organization, operation, and inter-relationships of the parties—is an integral part of its institutional structure." Other scholars find in the party-democracy linkage an easy guide to identifying democratic government. Mayo sees parties as one of the "touchstones" of a democratic system, while Dahl refers to the existence of parties as a "litmus paper test for the presence or absence of democracy in a country."[3] Even some who have disliked the idea of parties have accepted them as necessary evils. Lord Bryce, for instance, has stated:

> The three chief contributions which the United States has made to political science regarded as an Applied Science or Practical Art have been [written constitutions, courts of law to interpret those constitutions, and] the organization of political parties. Of these the first two are precautions against, or mitigations of, faults to which democracy is liable; while the third has proved to be an aggravation of those faults, undoing part of the good which the two former were doing, and impairing popular sovereignty itself. Yet party organization is a natural and probably inevitable incident of democratic government (1921: 27).

Ranney (1975: 46) refers to those American reformers who would agree with Bryce as "regulators" who have viewed parties as mischievous but "have accepted the propositions that parties are inevitable in a representative government that cherishes free speech and assembly."

Given the degree of importance attributed to political parties today, it is probably little wonder that there has been a well-documented concern with the question of how parties might be made "better," i.e., how the parties might maximize their utility for the society along one or another dimension of their activities. In pursuit of that end, "models" of parties and party systems have been developed with which existing parties may be compared and toward which they presumably should be altered. This concern with developing "proper" parties has been a topic of special interest to students and would-be reformers of the American parties, whose condition and prospects for change are major foci of this book.

ALTERNATIVE MODELS OF PARTIES IN DEMOCRACY

That there is no single viewpoint concerning the proper design for parties in democratic systems is readily apparent from the range of reforms that have been proposed for just the American parties in recent years. Programmatic or pragmatic, hierarchical or internally democratic, legally free or restricted—these are just examples of the alternative characteristics, all of which have been sought by reformers at one time or another. Choices among these alternatives reveal underlying conceptions of democracy and the party's role in it.

According to Robinson, most who are interested in party reform can be identified as either "revisionist" or "neo-classical" in democratic orientation:

> Whereas for revisionists, the central question for democratic government is how to reconcile the demand for participation with the need for "coherent, effective" government, for neo-classical democrats, the central question is how to stimulate personal and communal development (1979: 7).

Consequently, revisionists prefer hierarchical parties which provide democracy between but not within parties, while neo-classicists strive for democracy at all levels of decision making. To the revisionist, "parties need to have clearly defined membership, reasonably well articulated hierarchies, and a will to win" (Robinson, 1979: 16) but need not be overly concerned with accountability or programs. The neo-classicist, on the other hand, prefers the openness of primaries to the more controlled conventions and would ultimately prefer participation in worker movements and action groups to party activity.[4]

Among those who do see parties as valuable, Everson (1980) would distinguish between those of "competing teams" and those of "policy mandate" orientations. While holding steadfastly to the goal of democracy *among* strong parties, the "competing teams" advocates reject the need and even the desirability of democracy *within* the party and of commitment to principle. Those of the "competing teams" orientation would presumably agree with Schumpeter's definition of a party as a "group whose members propose to act in concert in the competitive struggle for political power" (1950: 283) without being preoccupied with doctrine.

The "policy mandate" orientation is central to the controversial document, *Toward a More Responsible Two-Party System*, which was published in 1950 as the Report of the Committee on Political Parties of the American Political Science Association (APSA). The Report's "Summary of Conclusions and Proposals" is reprinted as Appendix A to this book, and we will refer often to its recommendations for reforming the American party system. According to Everson's analysis, the APSA Report does not regard "competing teams" as sufficient for democracy:

> In this version, democracy results from the choice between two specific sets of policy alternatives presented by the parties in an electoral campaign. When a party receives an electoral majority, that constitutes a policy mandate. Consequently party cohesion is necessary to fulfill the mandate. Cohesion is also necessary for the opposition to provide a clear-cut alternative for the next election. An additional element of democracy may be added to the theory: the necessity for party members to participate in the formulation of the policy alternatives for the party program (1980: 10).

So while the APSA Report calls for stronger national parties, it goes beyond that to seek things which the "competing teams" school finds either unimportant or undesirable: a clearer choice of policy alternatives, greater party cohesion in the legislature, *and* democracy in the internal workings of the party.

Throughout the history of parties in America, tensions have existed among these major competing views of how the "proper" democratic party should look and act. And there has been no shortage of attempts to "reform" the parties in one or another of the directions suggested by these perspectives, as can be easily documented by a brief review of the history of American party reform.

REFORM EFFORTS IN THE UNITED STATES

Partly because Americans have never been completely satisfied with their party system and partly because parties are perceived to be among the more easily reformed of social institutions, there has been no shortage of attempts to make the American system work better by altering its parties (see Ranney, 1975: 209 ff. and Crotty, 1977: 193 ff.). The history of party reform in America has been a long and varied one.

Ranney (1975) argues that there have been three main "epochs" of party reform in the United States: the "Jacksonian" reforms (1820–1840), the "Progressive" reforms (1890–1920), and finally the period of "Modern" reforms (1952–?). The major objective of the Jacksonian reforms was to "open" the parties' method of selecting candidates; this was accomplished by abolishing the caucus and state-based methods in favor of the national convention. The basic goal of the Progressives, led by "Fighting Bob" La Follette of Wisconsin, was to place legal limitations on party affairs. Legal codes were established, nonpartisan municipal elections became a common practice, and the direct primary was favored as a less "controlled" means of selecting the party's delegates and candidates.

Since the early 1950s, Ranney suggests, there have been *two* major thrusts to party reform:

> The first has been the claim established by the national committees and conventions of both parties that they and not their state and local affiliates have the ultimate control over the membership of the national agencies. The second and more widely discussed thrust has been the efforts of both parties to make their procedures for selecting national convention delegates more open and the conventions more representative (1975: 19).

It would appear that these two thrusts are both consistent with the APSA Committee's goals, but it has been, in part, the Democratic party's experience with trying to achieve them simultaneously that has pointed up an inherent problem in the model itself.

Reforms intended to "nationalize" the party (e.g., national control over the national committee membership and the enforcement of national delegate selection rules) have raised questions about the place of such impositions in a "democratic" body, and the more numerous attempts to further democratize the party (e.g., greater usage of primaries and affirmative action in the selection of convention delegates) have had a chilling effect on the effort to make it more unified and programmatic. Schattschneider (1942: 58) had warned that "it is manifestly impossible for 27 million Democrats to control the Democratic Party," a warning that went largely unheeded as the party emphasized the "intraparty democracy" goal in its 1974 Charter (reprinted in full in Appendix B), while making only shallow attempts to implement the other goals of the APSA Committee Report.[5]

Not only may it be impossible to achieve effective parties that are both programmatically and electorally strong *and* internally democratic; but it is still an issue whether internal party democracy is even desirable, especially if it means abandoning the other "responsible party" objectives of the APSA Committee. After all, the parties have gone the route of greater internal democracy, and what has been the result? According to Ranney (1975: 194–5):

> Even more than in Schattschneider's day, American parties are incontestably the most open and internally democratic in the world. . . . Yet have these changes made our parties better instruments of democratic government than, say, the much more closed parties in other Western democracies? The leading scholar of comparative parties replies, in effect: different, yes; better, no [see Epstein, 1967: 111–129].

And no less an advocate of direct participation in presidential selection than Eugene McCarthy suggested in 1978 that party reforms had gone too far. Citing the lack of issue clarity and the inability of a President to garner support from his own party as stemming from the greater democratization, McCarthy took the position of favoring "party caucuses or conventions over state primaries in selecting presidential candidates—to ensure that party leaders have some say in the selection."[6]

Calls for *strengthening* the American parties have continued from within the political science community as well. The desire for stronger parties led a group of political scientists to establish in 1976 a "Committee on Party Renewal," which saw parties as indispensable to the realization of democracy. In 1980 these party scholars recommended a ten-point program for party renewal, which includes proposals for both procedural and organizational reform (see Appendix D).[7] Yet, while both parties have recently instituted some changes which might be considered at least *potentially* "nationalizing" (and which will be documented in Chapter 7), it remains the case that neither national party organization is "strong" today relative to either the parties of many other democracies or the "model" of the APSA Report.

The question of whether the parties should place the greater emphasis on internal democracy or strong organization may not be entirely academic. In addition to being ineffective programmatically, and perhaps as a result of it, the parties have found themselves in a condition described by some as "decline" and by others as "decay."[8] At the same time that the parties have become more "open" and "democratic," their support has declined markedly. In 1980 the percentage of eligible voters claiming to be "independents" was roughly double the comparable figure for 1950. While it is not our purpose here (as it is the purpose of others; for example, Crotty and Jacobson, 1980, and Ladd, 1978) to consider all of the possible causes for this sad state of party affairs, it does serve our purpose to suggest at least one possible cause. It is at least reasonable to argue (as does Broder, 1972) that the party decline is a result of the parties' unwillingness and/or inability to provide clear alternatives on the pressing national issues of the day and to solidify the party-in-government behind those alternatives. In short, the parties may be perceived as being unable to perform the functions that have served as the basis of their popular support in the past and as being largely irrelevant to the voters' needs today.

If one accepts that argument, then among the appropriate responses would be a number of the goals mentioned earlier: (1) establishment of a well-organized and hierarchical party structure, (2) provision of clear policy alternatives, and (3) unified performance of the party-in-government. But even advocates of these objectives, even those who perceive these reforms as critical to the parties' very survival, might well raise anew a question that has plagued such efforts in the past: Could the parties change in these ways, even if they wanted to, given the context in which they must operate?

THE ARGUMENT OF "ENVIRONMENTAL CONSTRAINTS"

Those who have argued for stronger American parties in the image of the British parties have continually been challenged by the question of whether such parties could be successfully imported into the American environment. It has widely been assumed that parties are, to some extent, the products of their context. Blondel (1969: 125), for instance, has argued that "in all cases, the influence of outside elements has played a part in the development or modification of internal [party] structures," and Lawson (1976: 27) has noted that "no political institution operates in a vacuum, political parties least of all."

If environmental effects are generally understood, they have been given special consideration by the students of American parties. Keefe, for instance, began his book on the American parties with this argument:

> Any attempt to unravel the mysteries of American political parties might well begin with the recognition of this fact: The parties are less what they make of themselves than what their environment makes of them. The parties are not free to develop in any fashion that they might like, to take on any organizational form that might appear desirable, to pursue any course of action that might seem to be required, or to assume any responsibility that might appear appropriate. The truth of the matter is that the shape of American parties is strongly influenced by the design of the legal-political system, the election system, the political culture, and the heterogeneous quality of American life. To a remarkable extent, the party system owes its form and substance to the impact of external elements (1972: 1).

And Banfield was no less emphatic in suggesting:

> With respect to the American party system, it seems obvious that the crucial features of the situation are all fixed. The size of our country, the class and cultural heterogeneity of our people, the number and variety of their interests, the constitutionally-given fragmentation of formal authority, the wide distribution of power which follows from it, the inveterate taste of Americans for participation in the day-to-day conduct of government when their interests are directly at stake—these are all unalterable features of the situation. Taken together, they mean that the party system can be reformed only within very narrow limits (1964: 26).

In fact, arguing along the line that we get the parties we deserve, Ranney has said that our governmental system is "designed to inhibit majority rule, and in such a system American parties, decentralized and irresponsible as they are, are entirely appropriate" (1954: 160).

Even those who have been most vocal in calling for stronger parties have accepted the limits placed on them by the environment but have argued for the change that may be possible within those limits. Schattschneider felt that the parties should rise above the federal and separation of powers systems to provide more national control over party affairs. And the APSA Committee's Report, while recognizing a value in the cabinet system of government, conceded that constitutional change "is not a practicable way of getting more effective parties," and instead challenged the parties to explore "the opportunities they have for more responsible operation under existing constitutional arrangements" (1950: 35–36).

Yet, with all of the importance that is generally attributed to the environment in shaping its parties and with the special importance the question may have for the ability of the American parties to strengthen themselves today, there has been no systematic assessment of the extent to which the parties are constrained by their environments and for what reasons. It is the purpose of this book to undertake such an assessment and, while doing so, to develop and test a set of theoretical underpinnings to explain the environment-party relationship.

Our primary purpose here is to shed light on the ability of the American parties to better approximate "strong" parties, *if they wish to.* The underlying theoretical questions guiding our research in the next several chapters are: To what extent does the environment set parameters on its parties' character, and why? Our answers will come from a systematic comparative analysis of a large number of competitive parties in democratic systems. In Chapter 2 we will discuss the research methods employed here. Then in Chapters 3 through 6 we will explore the effects of various environmental factors and the environment in general on the characteristics most often associated with the "responsible parties" model of strong parties: party ideology, degree of organization, centralization of power, and cohesion.[9] Finally, in Chapters 7 and 8 we will apply our earlier findings to the American situation and consider the extent to which the American setting might allow its parties to heed the call of the 1950 APSA Report:

Parties: Change Thyselves!

NOTES

1. At their genesis in Parliament in the seventeenth century, British "parties" were not the mass organizations that we usually think of today but instead were aristocratic factions which saw the need for "blocs" to organize legislative voting along lines consistent with their shared interests. Political organizations in Britain did not begin to serve the electoral function that we tend to associate with today's parties until a major extension of the suffrage occurred in 1867, which resulted in the need to educate and organize the mass of new voters.

2. For instance, Neil Reimer (1962: 109) merely views parties "as one of the heroes of modern democracy."

3. The above quotations are from E. E. Schattschneider (1942: 1), J. Roland Pennock (1979: 275), Peter Merkl (1980: 1), C. W. Casselini (1961: 20), H. B. Mayo (1960: 66), and Robert Dahl (1967: 203).

4. See Robinson (1979), pp. 16–17.

5. For an excellent account of party reforms, see Crotty (1977).

6. In Godfrey Sperling, "More Power to the . . . Party?" *Christian Science Monitor*, Vol. 8 (September 1978), p. 4.

7. Bibby (1980) draws a distinction between "procedural" reform and "organizational" reform as two alternative modes of party change undertaken by the Democratic and Republican parties recently. In Chapter 7 we will employ Bibby's distinction in documenting changes undertaken by the parties.

8. Those who have described the parties in such terms include Crotty and Jacobson (1980), Scott and Hrebenar (1979), Sorauf (1980), and Ladd and Hadley (1978).

9. Though, as we have noted, the APSA Committee also called for internal democracy in what has come to be called the "Responsible Parties Report," the term "responsible parties" is often associated only with the notion of strong and programmatic parties, without regard to internal democracy. That is how we will use the term in the remainder of this book.

2

Studying Environmental Effects on Parties

Given their social and political environment, is it *possible* to make American parties "responsible"? That is, can the United States support parties that (1) offer a choice in policy orientations, (2) are well organized, (3) are centralized, and (4) are cohesive in carrying out their policies? We will address this question in the course of considering the broader one: 'What is the effect of the environment on party ideology, complexity, power, and cohesion across nations?' We seek to understand the constraints, if any, that a country's environment imposes on its parties, with particular reference to the Untied States and the Democratic and Republican parties.

This chapter begins with a discussion of the theoretical model that directs this study. Then the data used in the cross-national analysis are described. In the last two sections the statistical techniques which are used first to detect environmental effects on party characteristics and then to account for those effects in more theoretical terms are explained.

THE BASIC THEORETICAL MODEL

This study assumes that party ideology, organization, decentralization, and cohesion can be explained by three classes of variables: (1) *system-level* factors, such as features of the environment, (2) *individual-level* factors, such as traits and actions of party leaders, and (3) *party-level* factors, or other party characteristics.[1] The basic model is diagramed in Figure 2.1, which shows the three factors as independent causes of some party characteristic, Y

FIGURE 2.1   Basic Model for Explaining Party Characteristics

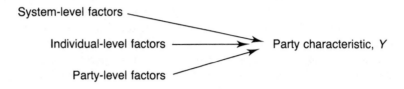

System-Level Factors

System-level factors are those physical, socioeconomic, and political features of the environment that set the framework for party politics in
every country. It is assumed that to be viable political forces, parties must
adjust to their environment. This assumption has two implications:
(1) parties within the same country come to resemble one another by
adapting to the same environment and (2) causal primacy resides in the
environment—it is the environment that shapes parties and not parties
that shape the environment. The first implication seems plausible and
testable. The extent to which parties resemble one another is clearly an
empirical question, answerable with appropriate data. The second implication, that the environment has causal primacy over party characteristics, is, on the whole, reasonable but not entirely accurate.

Clearly, parties have effects *on* their environment as well as being
affected *by* their environment. Party effects may be dramatic, even dis-
ruptive—as in a government overthrow, a ban on opposition groups, or
a forceful transformation of society. Such effects are more likely to issue
from "restrictive" or "subversive" parties than from the "competitive"
parties we will be studying. The model in Figure 2.1 obviously does not
account for such cases of party-induced change, where the ideology and
behavior of the party assume causal primacy over the political and even
cultural environment of the country.

Of course, parties can affect their environment in less dramatic ways
as well. Party effects may be subtle—as in establishing a program for
increased aid to education, thereby increasing the capabilities of the
population to participate in politics. Parties may also have more immediate effects—as in nationalizing the broadcast media. Whether long-term
or more immediate, all party effects on the environment are ignored by
the model in the interest of theoretical simplicity. We assume that, *in
the short run in democratic polities*, the causal primacy lies with the environment. (This assumption will be examined more closely below.)

Individual-Level Factors

Individual-level factors subsume such factors as activists' ideas that a
party ought to be formed in the first place, party leaders' views of

appropriate party strategy, and party dissidents' campaigns for new policy positions. In general, this class of factors provides for party formation
and for party change, which can occur even when the environment remains the same. Like system-level factors, individual factors have causal
primacy over party characteristics. But again, the issue of causality is
not clear-cut. For example, one can theorize that party defeat at the
polls is apt to spark changes in leaders' personalities and behaviors. Once
more, however, our model considers individual-level factors as causes of
party characteristics rather than as effects. In this case, the direction of
the cause-and-effect relationship does not bear directly on our analysis
or conclusions and so need not concern us further here.

Party-Level Factors

In a causally complex manner, some party characteristics are thought to
affect other party characteristics. For example, a party's ideological
orientation can be seen as a cause of its organizational structure, but its
structure is seldom regarded as a cause of its ideology. In other cases,
cause and effect are more difficult to disentangle: Is party ideology a
cause of electoral success, or does electoral success transform party
ideology? The establishment of causal primacy concerning various party-
level factors is a difficult theoretical challenge that must be resolved for
each combination of party characteristics. We will engage in such
theorizing in a limited way in Chapter 6, where we consider some party-
level causes of party cohesion.

THE ENVIRONMENT AND CAUSAL PRIMACY

Although the theoretical model in Figure 2.1 identifies three classes of
factors for explaining party characteristics, our attention focuses on only
one class of factors. We are interested only in system-level, or environmental, effects on party characteristics and not even all of these. Our
analysis will be limited to assessing environmental effects on party ideology, on the complexity of party organization, on the decentralization of
power within the organization, and on the cohesiveness in voting on
matters before the legislature.

It is helpful to examine the class of system-level (environmental)
factors more closely. As diagramed in Figure 2.2, three broad types of
environmental factors can be identified. There are *physical* factors, such
as the size, shape, and climate of the country. There are *socioeconomic*
factors, such as the racial and occupational composition of the society,
the degree of urbanization, and the educational level of its citizens.
Finally, there are *political* factors, such as the structure of the legislature, the type of electoral system, and the frequency of elections. For all

practical purposes, the physical features of a country's environment are immune to party-inspired attempts at change. Although socioeconomic characteristics are more changeable, they can be altered substantially as a result of party activities only in the long run.

FIGURE 2.2   The Party and the Spheres of Its Environment

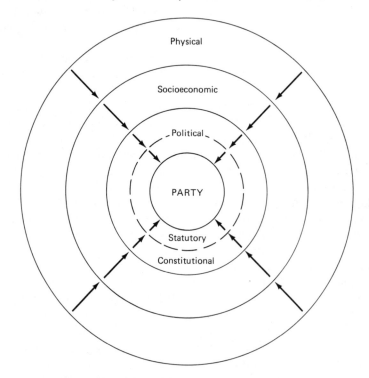

Features of the political environment vary in their susceptibility to change. On the relatively immutable side are the "constitutional" aspects of the governmental system that are deeply rooted in tradition. On the more changeable side are the "statutory" procedures specified by law but not embedded in the political culture. In the United States, the presidential form of government is a constitutional fixture that exerts a permanent influence on the operation of American political parties. The case of presidential government exemplifies the causal primacy of the environment over party characteristics, but there is a potential for party influence on other features of the political environment. For example, the election of United States representatives from single-member districts was required by an act of Congress in 1842. Under the pressure of party politics, Congress could presumably change the law and thereby alter the political environment to permit the election of representatives from multi-member districts. But single-member districts are so much a part of our political culture that change seems unlikely.

It is far more probable that Congress would change the political environment by providing for public funding of congressional election campaigns, as it did for presidential election campaigns beginning in 1976. Even more susceptible to change is the manner of selecting delegates to national party conventions. As a result of changes in state laws inspired by the Democratic party after its 1968 convention, the number of states holding primary elections for the Presidency increased from 15 to 35 in 1980. Clearly, this may be seen as an instance of parties' shaping their environment rather than being shaped by it, and thus it runs counter to the claim of causal primacy for the environment. Still, even changes in party-related statutes must take place within parameters that are established by the more permanent features of the environment (as indicated in Figure 2.2) and must appeal to a broader audience than the parties themselves. Hence, while parties may be able to "tune up" their environment to make it more receptive to particular party characteristics, that fine tuning must take place within a larger environment that is much less easily affected by party decisions. So, despite some exceptions to the theory, the physical, socioeconomic, and political environment may be seen as *causing* party characteristics rather than the other way around. We will return later to the possibility of altering the environment as a means of paving the way for change in the parties.

Our assessment of environmental effects will be based on a technique that enables us to estimate the "total association" between the environment and party characteristics. We will seek to account for this association by identifying environmental features that *explain* the association in theoretical terms. The proportion of the total association that we can explain theoretically will be the measure of our success in accounting for environmental influences. The variance in party characteristics that we *cannot* explain in our analysis we will attribute to either individual-level or party-level variables.

THE ENVIRONMENT AND PARTIES STUDIED

Our study of environmental effects on party characteristics extends across many parties and nations. It involves 95 political parties operating during 1957 to 1962 in 28 countries.[3] Although these countries could all be classified as "democracies" during the period of study, they represent many regions of the world and provide a wide variety of environments within which parties compete. Table 2.1 lists the countries included in the sample and the number of parties existing in each of these countries from 1957 to 1962.

TABLE 2.1   Polities in the Sample by Geo-Cultural Region* (with number of parties in parentheses)

Anglo-American Region
United States (2)
United Kingdom (2)
Australia (3)
Canada (4)
New Zealand (2)
Ireland (3)
India (2)

Western European Region
Austria (3)
France (5)
West Germany (3)
Greece (4)

Scandinavia and the Lowlands
Denmark (4)
Iceland (4)
Sweden (4)
The Netherlands (6)
Luxembourg (4)

South and Central America
Ecuador (5)
Peru (5)
Uruguay (2)
Venezuela (3)
Guatemala (4)[†]

Asia and the Far East
Burma (3)
Malaya (4)[†]

Africa and the Middle East
Lebanon (4)
Dahomey (3)
Kenya (2)
Turkey (2)
Uganda (3)

---

* Whether a polity was "democratic" was first determined by consulting Gurr's Polity Persistence and Change data set. For polities neither clearly democratic nor autocratic by those data, a polity was included in this reduced sample only if there was evidence of competitive elections during the 1957–62 time period.

† A fifth Guatemalan party, which followed primarily subversive tactics, was excluded from this sample, although Guatemala was still treated as a "five-party system" for other purposes. Likewise for Malaya, which was also treated as having five parties, although a subversive party was not included in the sample.

Although these data pertain to an earlier period, they constitute the only party data available for studying environmental effects on party characteristics. Moreover, general theories of environmental effects on parties are not bound to any particular time. For example, critics of the 1950 APSA Report argued that American parties could not become more cohesive to fit the responsible parties model because of the federal system and the presidential form of government. Although a country's environmental circumstances may change over time, any *theory* that relates federalism and presidentialism to party cohesion should hold for the 1980s as well as the 1950s. Because we will be testing general theories about the effects of environments on parties across nations, data from the late 1950s and early 1960s will serve as well as data from the 1980s. When we consider the specific case of environmental change over time in the United States in Chapter 7, we will update information on both the parties *and* the environment.

COUNTRY IDENTITY v. ENVIRONMENTAL FACTORS

The countries listed in Table 2.1 have parties that differ in many ways. For example, there are differences among parties in the degree of "institutionalization"—in their stability and permanence as features of the political landscape. Such differences might be reported in two contrasting styles: (1) parties in the United States are more institutionalized than those in Iceland, which are in turn more institutionalized than those in Turkey and especially in Kenya; or (2) the more modern the country, the more institutionalized its political parties. Both statements imply environmental effects on political parties, but one suggests the peculiarity of the country while the other translates the environmental effects into a general statement of relationship. Our goal in this book is to make general statements like the latter, but we will proceed by dealing first with particular observations like the former.

These two types of statements correspond to two opposing traditions in the logic of comparative inquiry (see Przeworski and Teune, 1970). The *idiographic* approach (from the Greek *idio* meaning "one's own") assumes that each country is cloaked with a peculiar environment, resulting from a certain combination of geographic, social, and historical factors, that produces a unique pattern of political institutions. This approach holds that one can understand a country's politics only by understanding the particular configuration of factors which make the country "the way it is." In contrast, the *nomothetic* approach (from the Greek *nomos* meaning "law") assumes that environmental differences can be analyzed for similarities and expressed in a set of variables incorporated into law-like explanations of environmental effects. Thus, one need not approach each country as a "unique" environment with definite and peculiar effects on its political institutions. Instead, every country's environmental features can be analyzed under the same theoretical framework.

Like all long-standing intellectual controversies, both the ideographic and nomothetic approaches contain more than an element of credibility. Surely no one would deny that each country is indeed unique —in the sense that there is no other exactly like it. On the other hand, every being in the universe is also unique in the same strict sense, yet we continually generalize about human existence, characteristics, and behavior. In their extreme forms, the idiographic approach denies any form of cross-national analysis while the nomothetic approach denies any limits on its powers of general explanation.

Fortunately, no scholar pursues these approaches in their extreme forms. The contemporary thrust in comparative politics is toward the nomothetic, but imperfections in knowledge inevitably force scholars to rely on idiographic explanations when all else fails. In practice, this leads to probabilistic statements such as "Modern countries are more

likely to have highly institutionalized parties." Exceptions to this generalization are sometimes explained away as deviant cases with reference
to particular country factors. It may be said, for example, that India has
parties that are more institutionalized than expected from its level of
modernity because of the influence of the British government or that
Greece has parties that are less institutionalized than expected because
of the emphasis on personalism in Greek politics.

To those who resort to particularized explanations of deviant cases,
the die-hard nomothetic comparativist would simply argue that the
search for underlying variables has not ended. Additional theoretical development could ultimately replace the reliance on proper names of
countries (e.g., "India," "Greece") in a satisfactory explanation.[4] Given
the problem at hand, determining the relative influence of environmental effects on party characteristics, the nomothetic comparativist suffers
under the special burden of not knowing when he has exhausted the explanatory potential of environmental factors. That is, assuming, according to our model, that environmental factors cannot explain all the
variations, how can one determine when the upper limit of environmental explanation is being approached?

An answer lies in the logic of the idiographic approach. This
approach contends that in some highly complex manner—so complex as
to defy ordinary attempts at analysis—hundreds of country-specific factors interact to produce a unique environmental setting for each political
system. Only through exhaustive configurative analysis for each country
can one understand the impact of its environment on its political institutions. As Braibanti describes configurative analysis:

> For each system we would have to list variable factors numbering into the
> thousands and perhaps more. The analysis would spiral through historical,
> economic, psychological, religious, and similar factors outward and down-
> ward until it encompassed all the known aspects of the social order....
> Ultimately we would be able to say that when a specified set of two or
> three hundred variable factors appear in a certain relationship, a specific in-
> stitutional manifestation or a specific function will also be found. When
> such a stage is reached, scientific political comparability will have come of
> age (1968: 52–53).

Denied this perfect state of knowledge, political scientists may have to
content themselves with simply observing the wondrous outcomes of the
unfathomable process by noting that parties in the United States are
more institutionalized than those in Iceland, which are, however, more
institutionalized than parties in Turkey and especially in Kenya, and so
on.

It is here that the logic of the idiographic approach can be used to
advantage in fashioning a theoretical explanation of environmental
effects on party characteristics. Let us temporarily accept the idiographic
reliance on the "uniqueness" of country environment in studying party

characteristics. That is, let us treat the country itself as a variable and examine the extent to which parties in the same country display the same characteristics. Whatever explanatory potential inheres in environmental factors under the theory of "environmental determinism" certainly should operate with maximum effect when the complete configuration of factors is represented by the country itself as the explanatory variable. By assessing the maximum effect of environmental factors on party characteristics—without knowing exactly what these factors might be other than "countryness"—we can fix the total association of the environment with party characteristics and thereby estimate the magnitude of environmental explanation. Rather than evaluating the potential contribution of the environment with reference to the unrealistic and theoretically inappropriate standard of 100 percent, we can obtain a more realistic estimate of the impact of the environment. The statistical procedure appropriate to this logical extension of the idiographic approach is the analysis of variance.

ASSESSING ENVIRONMENTAL EFFECTS WITH ANALYSIS OF VARIANCE

[*Authors' Note*: The following sections are designed especially for readers who are unacquainted with statistical methods. Those who are familiar with techniques of regression and analysis of variance may wish to read more lightly over the remainder of this chapter.]

Analysis of variance is a statistical technique for assessing the effect of a *qualitative* independent variable on a *quantitative* dependent variable. In our analysis, the country identity is the qualitative independent variable and the measures of party characteristics are the quantitative dependent variables. The basic idea underlying our analysis of variance is that if the country identity does affect a party characteristic, there will be relatively little variation, or "variance," among parties *within* a country compared to that *between* countries. In other words, strong environmental effects should cause all parties in the same country to demonstrate similar characteristics in comparison to parties in other countries.

Our measure of environmental effects is based on the statistical concept of "variance." In Figure 2.3, nine hypothetical parties (labeled by letters of the alphabet) are plotted along an ideological continuum from left to right. The continuum is arbitrarily scaled so that the midpoint is scored "0," the extreme leftist position is scored "−3," and the extreme rightist position is scored "+3."[5] Each party has a score according to its placement on the scale. The average score for these nine parties is 0. The total variation in party ideology scores is measured by subtracting the mean (0 in this example) from each score, squaring the difference, and summing the squared differences. "Variance" is merely the sum of squared differences divided by the number of cases (9 in this example). Sometimes it will be more convenient to analyze the *average* variation (variance), while other times we will use the *total* variation (the sum of the squared differences). The computation of the total variation of ideological scores among this set of parties is illustrated in Figure 2.3.

FIGURE 2.3   Example of Computing Variation among Nine Parties on a Hypothetical Left-Right Ideological Continuum

Positions of parties A to I on hypothetical continuum:

A	B	C		D		E		F		G	H	I
−3	−2.5	−2	−1.5	−1	−.5	0	+.5	+1	+1.5	+2	+2.5	+3
Left						Center						Right

Party	Ideology Score	−	Mean Score	=	Deviation	Squared Deviation
A	−3		0		−3	9
B	−2.5		0		−2.5	6.25
C	−2		0		−2	4
D	−1		0		−1	1
E	0		0		0	0
F	+1		0		+1	1
G	+2		0		+2	4
H	+2.5		0		+2.5	6.25
I	+3		0		+3	9

Total variation = Sum of squared deviations = 40.5

In this hypothetical example, the nine parties do vary in their ideological orientations. As shown in Figure 2.3, the amount of total variation around the mean ideology score is calculated to be 40.5. Our objective is to determine the extent to which the countries that these parties operate within can "explain" some or all of this variation.

Two models of country effect on party ideology are portrayed in Figure 2.4. In model 1, the nine parties are grouped into three hypothetical countries with systems of four, two, and three parties respectively. The average ideology score within each country is 0 (the same as the overall mean), and there is great variation in party ideology within each country. In fact, the sum of the country variations is equal to the total variation over all nine parties. Thus, model 1 shows no effect of country on party ideology. Model 2, on the other hand, reveals a pronounced clustering of "leftist" parties in country I,' "centrist" parties in country II', and "rightist" parties in country III'. Clearly, the country environment *does* have an effect on the ideological offerings of parties in model 2.

FIGURE 2.4 Graphic Displays of the Analysis of Variance Model for Evaluating the Effect of Country Identity on Party Ideology

Model 1: No Effect of Country on Party Ideology

	Country Average	Country Variation
Country I with 4 parties:	0	20.0
Country II with 2 parties:	0	12.5
Country III with 3 parties:	0	8.0
	Sum	= 40.5[a]

Model 2: Large Effect on Ideology

	Country Average	Country Variation
Country I' with 4 parties:	-2.1	2.2
Country II' with 2 parties:	+.5	.5
Country III' with 3 parties:	+2.5	.5
	Sum	= 3.2[b]

Ideological scale:

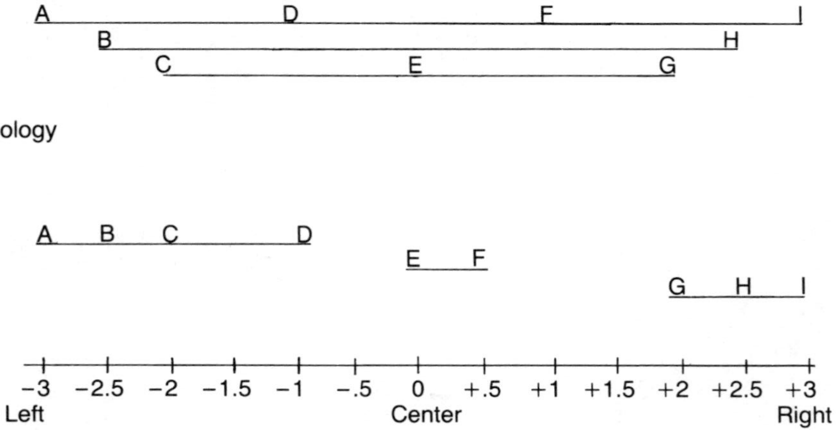

-3 -2.5 -2 -1.5 -1 -.5 0 +.5 +1 +1.5 +2 +2.5 +3
Left   Center   Right

[a] Because the average party ideology score within each country equals the mean score for all nine parties (see Figure 2.3), the sum of variations within countries (40.5) is equal to the total variation over all nine parties. Thus, country identity has no association with reduction of variation in party ideology.

[b] Because the parties tend to cluster by ideology within countries (as shown by the country averages and reduced variation), the sum of variations within countries (3.2) is much less than the total variation over all parties (40.5). The ratio of the amount of variation *within* countries to the *total* variation (3.2/40.5 = .08) measures the percentage of "error" in predicting party ideology from knowledge of country. By inference, if we have 8 percent "error," then we are "explaining" 92 percent of party ideology by country identity.

The effect of country on party ideology can be assessed by a statistic called E^2. The measure can be computed in various ways. We use the formula which views the sum of "within" country variation as the amount of "error" in predicting to party ideology from country identity. (If parties in the same country differ in ideology, the *country* cannot possibly explain their differences; hence, variation within countries reflects error in explanation.) The formula then subtracts this "within" variation from the "total" variation to yield the "explained" variation. Thus,

$$E^2 = \frac{\text{Total variation} - \text{Within variation}}{\text{Total variation}} = \text{Explained variation}$$

The E^2 values for models 1 and 2 are calculated as:

Model 1:
$$\frac{40.5 - 40.5}{40.5} = 0$$

Model 2:
$$\frac{40.5 - 3.2}{40.5} = .92$$

By reference to the E^2 statistics, we can say that country identity has no effect on party ideology in model 1 but that country "explains" 92 percent of the ideological differences among all nine parties in model 2. Throughout the book, we will assess country effects on party characteristics by reporting the E^2 statistics computed across all 95 parties grouped by countries.[6]

The analysis can be illustrated by assessing country effects on real (rather than hypothetical) data on party ideology. The next chapter describes a scale for measuring party ideology concerning the government's role in the economy. Without explaining that measure here, we can report the way the parties in each of the 28 countries fall along the ideological scale. In fact, parties in most countries range rather widely across the scale, conforming more to model 1 (no country effect) than model 2 (large effect). (A look ahead at Figure 3.2 on page 29 will substantiate this claim.) The actual E^2 statistic for the distribution of party positions is only .29, indicating that less than one-third of the variation in party ideology is associated with country environment. While some countries contained parties with similar ideologies in the 1957–62 period (e.g., India, Uruguay, Dahomey, Kenya, and Uganda), most countries (even the United States) had parties that differed more substantially in their policy positions. Thus, as assessed by E^2, the country environment has only a small effect on the ideological positions of its individual parties. As we will see in the next chapter, however, the country environment has a much stronger effect on the ideological nature of the party *system*.

EXPLAINING ENVIRONMENTAL EFFECTS
WITH REGRESSION ANALYSIS

Detecting country effects with the E^2 statistic is only the first step in explaining environmental effects on party characteristics. Once we know the magnitude of the total association between country identity and a given party characteristic through E^2, we can depart from the idiographic approach and search for a nomothetic, or theoretical, explanation of how the environment affects political parties. Our search will begin by identifying social and political factors that scholars have cited as causes of party ideology, complexity, decentralization, and cohesion. The effects of environmental factors on these party characteristics will be measured using simple correlational analysis.

The correlations will be measured by the coefficient, r, which varies from $+1.0$ to -1.0.[7] Coefficients tending toward 0 indicate the absence of a relationship. Coefficients tending toward positive or negative 1.0 indicate a very strong relationship. The sign simply tells whether the relationship is direct or inverse. The absolute value indicates the magnitude of the correlation. Squaring the coefficient (r^2) expresses the percentage of variance in one variable that is "explained" by the other. By correlating each environmental factor with the party characteristics, we will determine what proportion of the country effects we can recapture by single-cause theories. If any single cause is sufficiently powerful, we should be able to approach the variation explained by country identity.

Because we live in a social world of many causes, however, we should not expect too much from single-factor theories. It is likely that no single factor will explain much variation in any party characteristic, and we will need to consider factors in combination rather than in isolation. The technique we will use is multiple regression. This analytical model assumes that any number of independent variables combine in an additive fashion to affect a single dependent variable. Multiple regression analysis computes the optimum combination of the independent variables in the sense that the resulting equation yields predicted values for the dependent variable that correlate higher with the actual values than would the values predicted by any other equation involving the same set of independent variables. The square of the resulting multiple correlation coefficient, represented by R^2, expresses the proportion of variance in the dependent variable that can be explained by the independent variables, taken together simultaneously. Multiple regression allows us to estimate the joint effects of several environmental variables acting on each party characteristic. Moreover, it enables us to estimate the relative contributions of each factor to the overall explanatory power of the multivariable explanation.

The mathematics of multiple regression need not be explored in any depth here, for that is properly the subject of statistics texts. But it is necessary to sketch the form of the regression equation produced from a regression analysis. As we employ the technique, the regression equation is of this form:

$$Y = b_1X_1 + b_2X_2 + b_3X_3 \ldots + b_nX_n$$

where: Y = the dependent variable to be explained
X_i = the independent factors used to explain Y
b_i = the *weights* for the corresponding factors

Regression analysis computes the optimum weights for the independent explanatory factors, such that they add together to make the best possible prediction of the dependent variable, Y. These weights are reflected in the b values, which are also known as the *regression coefficients*. In our usage, each coefficient can be interpreted as expressing the amount of change in the dependent variable due to a change of one (standardized) unit in any explanatory variable while holding the others constant. It is a common practice to exclude variables which do not add appreciably to the overall explanation from the multivariable explanatory model, and a similar practice will be followed here.[8]

In the chapters to come, multiple regression will be employed for the purpose of estimating the ability of a number of environmental factors, when combined, to account for variation in party ideology, organization, decentralization, and cohesion. We begin in Chapter 3 to analyze the effects of environment on party ideology.

NOTES

1. This view of causal factors conforms to one in the literature on organizational theory. See S. B. Sells, "Toward a Taxonomy of Organizations," in W. W. Cooper, H. J. Leavitt, and M. W. Shelly, II, (eds.), *New Perspectives in Organization Research* (New York: Wiley, 1964), pp. 515–532.

2. This diagram is not intended as a complete causal model; arrows which might be included to represent "indirect effects" are deleted in order to simplify the presentation. An underlying assumption of this book is that any indirect effects would be small relative to the direct effects.

3. These parties and countries were selected from a broader sample of 147 parties in 53 countries studied in the International Comparative Political Parties (ICPP) Project. See Kenneth Janda, *Political Parties: A Cross-National Survey* (1980a). The broader sample included parties and countries of all types, providing a representative sample of the world's party systems. Because our present theoretical framework is limited to environmental effects within "democratic" countries on "competitive" parties, we have excluded from the analysis 47 "restrictive" and "subversive" parties and 5 competiitive parties struggling to exist in countries that were nondemocratic during the time period 1957–62. The ICPP data pertain to the parties as they existed during that time period.

4. Przeworski and Teune hold that "the role of comparative research in the

process of theory building and theory testing consists of replacing proper names of social systems by the relevant variables" (1970: 30).

5. Those who consult *Political Parties: A Cross-National Survey* (Janda, 1980a), the source of these data, should note that we have reversed the signs of the party scores for the issue orientation variables to facilitate the left-right spatial presentation.

6. This use of E^2 might be challenged on several grounds. First, some may wonder whether the nature of the judgmental coding may itself contribute to the size of E^2, so that coders might be biased toward giving similar codes to parties in the same country. Safeguards against such a bias were built into the coding process. Independent codes were produced by pairs of coders for many of the variables, with an additional check of the data by area experts. There is also empirical evidence that coder "set" alone could not account for large E^2s. If that were true, the E^2 would be large for all the concepts in the ICPP project. However, many of them are small, including the E^2 reported in this chapter for ideological position.

Second, it should be noted that there is a potential for bias to result from using the E^2 statistic with the small numbers of cases in the analysis of variance categories used in this study. When cases in a category constitute a very small sample of the population of cases fitting the category requirements, there is a tendency for the sample within-category variance to underestimate the population within-category variance. When the category n's are small, the denominator of the E^2 formula (i.e., the total variance) is underestimated. Since the numerator (i.e., the between-category variance) is not similarly influenced by the category n's, the overall E^2 is biased upward. However, since the parties in the countries studied constitute *populations* rather than samples (i.e., a four-party system is represented by all four parties), we have the population within-category variance rather than a sample-based estimate subject to small-n bias. Hence, E^2 is an accurate reflection of explained variance in this analysis.

7. We will be employing the familiar Pearson product-moment coefficient in our correlational analysis.

8. In presenting results of the regression analysis, we will employ a decision rule that enables us to (1) adequately assess the total combined explanatory power of the selected set of explanatory variables while (2) fairly assessing the statistical significance and relative magnitudes of the independent contributions of individual variables. We report the regression results for that equation whose "adjusted R^2" is largest for the given set of independent variables. The unadjusted R^2 will always increase, however slightly, with the addition of variables to the analysis. The adjusted R^2 corrects for the addition of independent variables. Thus when the adjusted R^2 begins to decline with the addition of new variables, the variables being added do not "carry their own weight" and will not be regarded as improving the explanation. For a discussion of the adjustment to R^2, see Gordon Hilton (1976), pp. 153–154.

3

The Environment and Party Ideology

INTRODUCTION

In 1950 a group of American political scientists took a look at the British parties, liked what they saw (or at least what they thought they saw), and wrote a Report suggesting the potential benefits of transporting "party responsibility" to the United States. Among the longed-for prescriptions for the American system was more "programmatic" parties, i.e., parties offering a clear choice among clearly stated programs. As they put it:

> Popular government in a nation of more than 150 million people requires political parties which provide the electorate with a proper range of choice between alternatives of action (APSA, 1950: 15).

But what existed instead was a situation where the "alternatives between the parties are defined so badly that it is often difficult to determine what the election has decided even in the broadest terms" (APSA, 1950: 3). If the party labels are to act as meaningful surrogates for policy alternatives, they argued, and particularly if they are to facilitate rational voting, then the parties must make clear what those labels stand for and that they stand for things that are different.

Since publication of the Report, numerous critics have argued that, even if more "ideological" or "programmatic" parties were desirable, they would not be electorally acceptable in this country. Environmental limitations on the ideological nature of the American parties are usually assumed to include the plurality electoral system, the number of parties (i.e., only two), and the lack of a sharp and deep ideological division within the society, which might promote ideologically distinct parties. Such an environment might not only allow but perhaps would even require that the American parties be "pragmatic" rather than "ideological," i.e., that they employ very similar and perhaps internally inconsistent approaches to issues if they hope to win national elections.

Though the programmatic clarity of the American system could presumably be enhanced if (1) one or both of the parties deviated farther from the ideological "middle of the road" and/or (2) one or both of the parties developed a set of general "principles" from which individual issue positions could be easily deduced, it is possible that the environment would prohibit either of these things from happening. It is the major purpose of this chapter to investigate the effects of a number of social and political factors upon (1) the ability of a system to produce an ideologically "extreme" (or at least, "non-centrist") party, (2) the ability to produce a "consistent" party, and (3) the range of "choice" that the system provides to its voters.

Our approach is to begin by determining the extent and sources of environmental effects upon party ideology across our full sample of countries, and then to employ these findings in analyzing the American situation. But first, we turn to a more general discussion of party ideology and our attempt to measure it.

"IDEOLOGY": THE LEFT-RIGHT DIMENSION

Before setting out to measure "choice," we must first establish: "choice on what dimension?" Given a common definition of ideology as "a general value structure and immediate political goals" (Gross, 1974: 78), there are obviously many alternative ideologies that might serve as the object of our measure. We have chosen to use the left-right continuum here because it appears to have been the most widely relevant ideological scale during the period for which we have data (1957–62) and hence is the most useful for our comparative analyses.

By Duverger's historical account of ideological development in Western Europe, the first half of the nineteenth century was dominated by another political conflict, between the "liberals" and "conservatives," over the issues of liberty, equality, and mass participation in politics. But as the bourgeoisie won their rights and liberties from the aristocracy, that line of combat was replaced by a new set of issues emphasizing the economic struggle between workers and owners. This conflict would continue into the twentieth century, with socialists seeking government guarantees of an end to the "exploitation of the worker" opposed by capitalists decrying any governmental role in the economy as both unnatural and unwise. From this perspective, then, the liberal/conservative conflict was largely resolved in Western Europe long before the period of our data and had been replaced by the left/right "economic" conflict.

Although Duverger's historical account is limited to Europe, the relevance of the left-right continuum is far more general. Duverger himself has argued:

> European political struggles of the nineteenth century established, at least in part, the ideological frameworks within which the main political struggles of today unfold. The study of European political parties provides the best foundation for understanding all political parties (1972: 39).

And Sartori (1976: 78), in his own analysis of party ideology, notes that "what compels us to utilize the left-right identification and ordering is a formidable reason, namely, that this appears to be the most detectable and constant way in which not only mass publics but also elites perceive politics."[1]

In restricting our analyses to only the left-right continuum, two caveats must be kept in mind. First, we agree with those who would argue that there are many additional ideological dimensions of party conflict that go unrepresented here. Given the impossibility of including all potential bases of party ideology, however, we have opted for the alternative of covering only the most widely applicable and hence the most meaningful for cross-national comparison. Second, some might question the relevance of even the left-right continuum to today's politics, arguing that that dimension has now gone the way of the earlier liberal/conservative conflict.[2] However, most studies of party policies and voters' perceptions of party policies conducted in the 1960s and early 1970s found that the left-right dimension continued to dominate distinctions among parties. (See the studies of dimensional analyses reported in Budge, Crewe, and Farlie, 1976.) Since our data cover the 1957–62 period and because our concern in using those data is more theoretical than descriptive, information about the left-right positions of the parties in that period should serve us adequately.

MEASUREMENT OF PARTY IDEOLOGY

Among the most important indicators of a party's orientation to the left-right continuum are its positions on four issues involving the government's role in the economy: whether the public or the private sector should be the principal owner of the means of production, whether the government should have a role in long-term planning of the economy, whether the government should take responsibility for programs of social welfare, and whether there should be a governmental program of redistributing the wealth. As indicated in Figure 3.1, we have such information for the parties in our data set. For each issue, each of the parties was given a score ranging from −5 to +5, with high positive scores indicating a "rightist" position in opposition to a governmental role in the economy and large negative scores indicating a "leftist" orientation in favor of governmental intervention.[3] Those scores served as the "raw" data from which more elaborate measures were constructed.

FIGURE 3.1   ICPP Left/Right Issue Variables

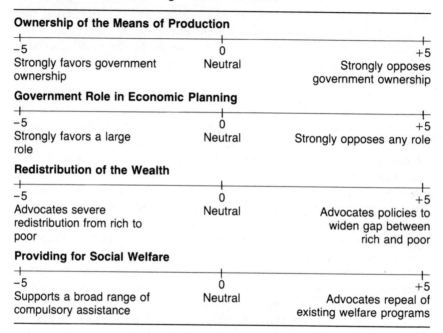

Ownership of the Means of Production

−5	0	+5
Strongly favors government ownership	Neutral	Strongly opposes government ownership

Government Role in Economic Planning

−5	0	+5
Strongly favors a large role	Neutral	Strongly opposes any role

Redistribution of the Wealth

−5	0	+5
Advocates severe redistribution from rich to poor	Neutral	Advocates policies to widen gap between rich and poor

Providing for Social Welfare

−5	0	+5
Supports a broad range of compulsory assistance	Neutral	Advocates repeal of existing welfare programs

Specifically, we are concerned here with the extent to which the environment might affect three different concepts that are related to the notion of clear ideological "choice" in a party system. Ideological *extremism* taps the degree to which the party's mean ideological thrust departs from the "center" of the left-right scale. Ideological *consistency* taps the degree to which a party (at a given point in time) takes ideologically consistent positions on the set of left-right issues. And ideological *distance* is simply the distance between the mean thrusts of the system's two parties which are farthest apart on the left-right continuum. As such, "distance" is a gross indicator of the range of ideological choice provided by the system.[4]

Our measures for all of these variables are based on the parties' raw positions on the four left-right issues. First, the party's ideological *position* is computed as the arithmetic mean (or "average") of the four issue scores. The positions for the parties in our sample, computed in this manner, are indicated by country in Figure 3.2.

FIGURE 3.2 Left/Right Positions of Parties

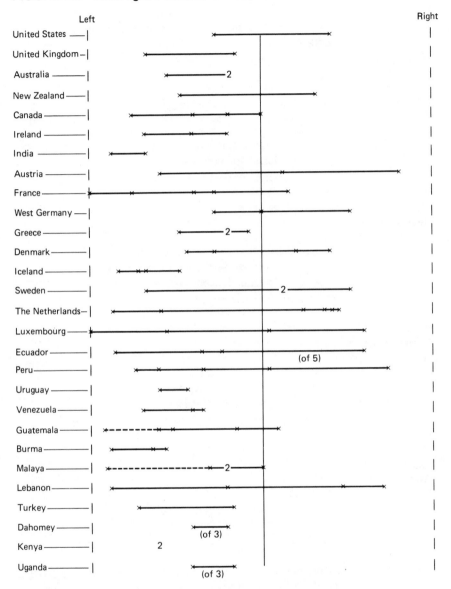

Once the party's position is ascertained, the *extremism* of the party can be measured as the simple distance of the party from the ideological "center" (i.e., as the absolute value of the party's position, since the "center" is zero on our scale). The *consistency* of the party's program is then measured as the average deviation of the individual issue positions from their mean (i.e., the average of the differences of the individual

FIGURE 3.3 Examples of Various Combinations of Extremism and Consistency

	Leftist	Center	Rightist
Production	X		
Planning	X		
Redistribution	X		
Welfare	X		

French Communist party:
leftist and consistent

	Leftist	Center	Rightist
Production	X		
Planning	X		
Redistribution		X	
Welfare	X		

Icelandic Social Democratic party:
leftist and inconsistent

	Leftist	Center	Rightist
Production		X	
Planning		X	
Redistribution		X	
Welfare		X	

Malayan Chinese Association:
centrist and consistent

	Leftist	Center	Rightist
Production		X	
Planning		X	
Redistribution		X	
Welfare	X		

Australian Liberal party:
centrist and inconsistent

issue scores from the party's over-all *position*).[5] Illustrations of parties with combinations of various degrees of extremism and consistency are provided in Figure 3.3, indicating that extremism need not imply consistency, and vice versa. Finally, the system's ideological "distance" is measured as the arithmetic difference between the ideological position scores for the two parties which are "farthest apart," i.e., the distance between the system's two "most different" parties. The distances are indicated by the connecting lines in Figure 3.2.

EXPLAINING ENVIRONMENTAL EFFECTS ON PARTY IDEOLOGY

Among the environmental factors most often suggested as determinants of party ideology are two related characteristics of the political system— the *nature of the electoral system* and the *number of political parties.*[6] Both the individual party's ideological consistency and the system's diversity are linked to the difference in electoral considerations between two-party and multi-party systems and between majority (or plurality) and proportional representation (P.R.) electoral systems. As argued by Hermens (1938), Duverger (1964b: 224–226), and others, proportional representation provides more electoral rewards to the "weaker" parties in the system than does the majority form of election, which makes it more difficult for "ideological" parties to survive. As Hermens (1938: 25) put it, "If P.R. gives to these radical groups, under normal conditions, only a comparatively small number of seats, it at least contributes greatly towards keeping them alive; whereas under the majority system, they sustain failure after failure, with the result that they tend to disappear completely from the political scene." Concerning the number of parties in the system, Mayer (1972: 227) argues that "principled parties thrive best in multi-party situations, where success can be based upon appeal to a fixed and ideologically homogenous clientele; [whereas] parties in two-party systems are forced to aggregate a more diverse clientele because political success consists of winning a plurality of the total vote." One reason for expecting a number/ideology relationship is the link between the nature of the electoral system and the number of parties, with the likelihood of having only two parties and hence of having only nonprogrammatic parties dropping precipitously with the shift from majority elections to proportional representation. But that linkage is not the only reason for expecting the number/ideology relationship. Sartori (1966: 159) has summarized a more direct reason: "The rule of thumb appears to be that the more numerous the parties, the less they can afford a pragmatic lack of distinctiveness." By this argument, increasing the number of parties, even within the same type of electoral system, should provide an incentive for increasing the range of choice provided by the parties.

Also likely to improve the lot of more "ideological" parties is the *probability of rule by a coalition government* and with that the increasing potential for such parties to participate in the government. As Schlesinger (1968: 434) argues, "Where the governing responsibility is shared or obscure, parties can govern and [also] retain a doctrine which has little relevance to the governing experience." And to extend Hermens's argument concerning the importance of a small party's gaining legislative *seats*, we might argue that participating in a coalition government, even as the weakest partner, would contribute greatly to the survival rate of what he calls "radical" parties.

A somewhat different type of governmental explanation for ideological "diversity" has been sugggested by Sigelman and Yough (1978: 374), who found substantial empirical support for the argument that *regime tolerance of opposition* "allows opposition parties of divergent ideological stripes to attract relatively large numbers of voters," while party systems in more restrictive regimes are "far less likely to polarize along left-right lines." While their dependent variable, polarization, includes the magnitude of "support" for parties of different ideologies and not just their placement on the ideological continuum, we find that both their argument and their findings warrant the inclusion of regime tolerance as a potential source of explanation in this study. The same regime intolerance that would deny support to a party of a particular ideological ilk could also make it difficult or impossible for such a party to exist in the system, thereby limiting the range of choice provided there.

So there are good theoretical reasons for expecting the type of electoral system, the number of parties, the potential for coalition participation, and the degree of regime tolerance of opposition to be related to the diversity of party ideologies in a system, and particularly to the existence of "ideological" parties within the system. For our analyses, each country is assigned a value on each of these variables. For the type of electoral system, Blondel's (1969) six categories are reduced to two for our purposes, with each country labeled as "proportional" or "plurality."[7] The number of parties is simply the number important enough to be studied by the ICPP project (as listed in Table 2.1). The probability of coalition government is measured as the percentage of the years from 1946 to 1956 during which coalition governments existed in the country. And regime tolerance of opposition is measured (as suggested by Sigelman and Yough, 1978: 365) as a composite score based on measures of interest aggregation, the role of police, press freedom, and the number of government sanctions imposed from 1960–1967. Together, these variables are employed to represent the "political/governmental" environment of the parties.

But to consider only political and governmental variables as sources of environmental explanation would be to ignore another important sphere of the environment: namely, the socioeconomic environment. For the study of party ideology, the most relevant features of the socioeconomic environment are those related to inequality within the society.

Milnor (1969: 104–5) has argued that "only in a *sharply divided society* is there a possibility of an ideological party forming," and only then if the division yields groups with well-developed self-identification and "a clear sense of separation from other interests in the society that may be potentially competitive or opposing" (emphasis added). Such groups, if they were to have relevance to the past several decades, were most likely to arise in societies that might be described as "unequal," where large social groups were left without their proportionate share of the opportunities and rewards that the systems had to offer. For this reason, we have included as a "socioeconomic" independent variable an indicator of the inequality of rewards among the various occupational "sectors" of the society. And because Milnor's "sharp societal divisions" are increasingly less likely to occur in more affluent societies, the gross national product per capita is also included as an independent variable (labeled "affluence" hereafter).[8]

The above set of arguments will serve as the theoretical foundation for the analyses which are to follow here. These analyses will differ from those which will follow in Chapters 4 through 6, in that here we will focus on explaining characteristics of the "party system" rather than features of the individual parties, as will be the case in the remaining chapters. The reason is quite simple: there are good reasons why the expected relationships would *not* hold at the level of the individual party. While it may be expected that *every* party in a plurality, two-party system would be pragmatic, for instance, it is hardly to be expected that *every* party in a proportional representation, multi-party system would be ideologically consistent and extreme. It might be expected, instead, that the parties in such a system would take a variety of positions on the left-right scale and display a range of attention to consistency. If that is the case (and it is, according to our data), then we would not expect significant relationships to exist between the environmental factors and our ideology variables at the *party* level. (This would explain our finding in Chapter 2 that only 29 percent of the variance in party-level ideological position can be explained by the environment.)

We would, however, expect those relationships to hold at the level of the party "system," where the theory is actually much more applicable. Stated generally, our expectations are that (1) the extremity of the "most extreme" party of a system will rise as the environment becomes more conducive to "extreme" parties, (2) the consistency of the "most consistent" party in the system should increase as the environment better approximates one conducive to "principled" parties, and (3) the range of choice, measured here as ideological "distance," should rise with proportional representation, multiple parties, coalition government, inequality, etc.[9] [It should be noted that we are using the term "environment" rather loosely in the remainder of this chapter, since we are now explaining *system*-level ideological variables with other factors that vary at the same level (such as number of parties).]

Table 3.1 presents the bivariate correlation coefficients for the relationships between the explanatory variables and the three system-level ideological variables. Though several of the expectations (and especially those related to tolerance and affluence) are not fulfilled, other arguments are supported by these results. Although none of the independent variables are significantly correlated with consistency, more of the propositions are supported for extremism and ideological distance. The most consistent support seems to be for the general argument that the political structure of the party system affects the range of choice that its parties can provide. Larger numbers of parties, proportional representation, and a higher propensity to form coalition governments are all significantly associated with greater *extremism* of the system's most non-centrist party and larger *distance* between the system's most different parties.

TABLE 3.1   Bivariate Correlations between System-Level Ideology Variables and Environmental Variables

	Extremism[a]		Consistency[b]		Distance[a]	
	r	*r²*	*r*	*r²*	*r*	*r²*
Coalition Propensity	.50*	.25	−.11	.01	.42*	.18
Number of Parties	.50*	.25	.30	.09	.65*	.42
Electoral System	−.33*	.11	.30[wd]	.09	−.40*	.16
Tolerance of Opposition	−.12[wd]	.01	−.08[wd]	.01	.24	.06
Sectoral Inequality	.32*	.10	.33	.11	.02	.00
Affluence	−.20	.04	.00	.00	.20[wd]	.04

[wd] Correlation is in opposite direction from that expected.
[a] N's equal 28 for extremism and distance correlations, except coalition ($n = 26$), sectoral inequality ($n = 25$), and affluence ($n = 26$).
[b] N's equal 27 for consistency correlations, except coalition ($n = 25$), sectoral inequality ($n = 24$), and affluence ($n = 26$). Dahomey was excluded from the consistency analysis, with none of its parties having the minimum requirement of three valid issue scores in order to assign a consistency score. Five other parties also failed to meet the minimum, one each in Greece, Luxembourg, Ecuador, Venezuela, and Uganda.
* Correlation is significant at the .05 level.

Since the three significant "political structure" variables, in particular, are related to one another as well as to the range of ideological choice, we would most likely exaggerate the combined influence of the variables if we were simply to sum the individual explained variances. However, the technique of "multiple regression" (see Chapter 2) enables us to determine more accurately the effects of a number of variables acting jointly on the ideological variables. The technique involves computing the optimum combination of the explanatory variables, yielding a regression coefficient for each variable which revels its relative importance in the final predictive equation (or "law"). Each coefficient can be interpreted as the amount of change in the dependent variable resulting from a change of one (standardized) unit in that particular independent variable while holding the others constant. (See Chapter 2).

COMBINED EXPLANATION

The "independent" and combined effects of the selected environmental factors upon the ideological variables are presented in Table 3.2. While the ability to explain "consistency" remains somewhat problematic, the combined explanation produces more satisfying results for the extremism and distance variables. Over one-third of the variance in "extremism" can be explained by the number of parties, coalition propensity, and sectoral inequality. And nearly one-half of the variance in "distance" can be explained by the number of parties and the nature of the electoral system alone (with slightly more variance explained with the addition of affluence, though in the opposite direction from that anticipated).

TABLE 3.2[a] Multiple Regression for System-Level Ideology Variables with Environmental Variables

	Standardized Regression Coefficient
Extremism with	
Number of Parties	.28
Coalition Propensity	.31
Sectoral Inequality	.20
$R^2 = .35$ Adjusted $R^2 = .26$ $N = 28$	
Consistency with[b]	
Sectoral Inequality	.43*
Electoral System	.44[wd]*
Number of Parties	.32
Affluence	.34[wd]
$R^2 = .36$ Adjusted $R^2 = .25$ $N = 27$	
Distance with[c]	
Number of Parties	.60*
Electoral System	−.19
Affluence	.17[wd]
$R^2 = .50$ Adjusted $R^2 = .43$ $N = 28$	

[wd] Regression coefficient is in opposite direction from that expected.

[a] The results given are for the equation whose adjusted R^2 is the largest among those possible with combinations of the nine independent variables. (See Chapter 2, note 8, for a discussion of the decision rule by which some variables were excluded from the regressions.) All R^2 are significant at the .05 level. Mean values are substituted for missing values of the independent variables.

[b] Without the variables whose coefficients are in the wrong direction, the overall R^2 is .15 for the equation involving only sectoral inequality (beta = .25) and number of parties (beta = .23).

[c] Without the variable whose coefficient is in the wrong direction, the overall R^2 is .47 for the equation involving only number of parties (beta = .58) and electoral system (beta = −.23).

* Significant at the .05 level.

Though our analyses also suggest that just over one-third of the variance in consistency can be jointly explained by four of the explanatory variables, the interpretation of these results is somewhat problematic. Though we expected plurality elections and affluence to make ideological consistency more difficult, our findings suggest that under the *ceteris paribus* conditions imposed by the multiple regression technique, they tend toward *greater* consistency. Perhaps it is because more affluent societies also tend to be industrialized societies, with parties organized to represent the interests of workers (or the working class), that we find affluence predicting to the presence of more, rather than less, consistent parties; that would also explain the unexpected positive (but small) relationship between affluence and ideological distance. And as for the electoral system, the very least that can be said is that plurality elections do not act as the severely restricting force on consistency that it has often been thought to be. We must offer one important caveat to all of the findings related to consistency, however: by measuring consistency across only the four very similar economic issues, we have severely limited the range of *possible* inconsistency. Hence, different findings might be forthcoming from analyses employing a measure based on a larger (and broader) set of issues; in other words, our findings might be limited to our particular choice of continuum and issues.

We feel more confident in concluding, on the basis of our analyses, that the environment does affect the extent to which parties may approach one or another of the ideological poles. Although, as is evident from Figure 3.2, it is not necessary for both parties in two-party systems to be as "middle-of-the-road" as the two American parties, it does appear that the truly "extremist" parties are limited to the multiparty systems and especially to those prone to government by coalition. The range of ideological choice provided by a party system, as measured by the distance between its two most different parties, also seems to be profoundly affected by other features of the environment (and especially the political environment) within which the parties operate.

Of special importance to the American parties is our finding that two-partyism and plurality elections tend to limit the range of choice provided by a party system. At first glance, this might be taken as empirical evidence that the very similar American parties are exactly what must be expected and perhaps are even best suited to such a system. But there is still the nagging comparison with the British system— similar to the American in electoral system and number of parties— which presumably has provided much clearer choices, even within that limiting environment. We turn now to an empirical assessment of the accuracy of that age-old comparison, in hopes of ultimately casting some light on the ability and the likelihood of the American parties to offer a clearer programmatic choice.

ANALYZING THE AMERICAN PARTIES: THE BRITISH COMPARISON

America's two main parties have long been critized for providing the voters with too little choice. The criticism perhaps culminated in the APSA Committee's Report in 1950, in which the American parties were compared to the British parties and found wanting. In spite of Britain's two-party system and majority elections, the proponents of the Report argued, the more "responsible" British parties still provide their voters with clear (or at least clearer) programmatic differences. The American parties, on the other hand, seldom provide meaningful differences in their platforms, which better approximate hodgepodges of issue stands than consistent programs.

Though our data refer to a slightly later period (1957 to 1962 rather than 1950), they bespeak a comparison of British and American parties supportive of Butler's reaction to the Report:

> The choice may seem more confused in the United States, but it is more far-reaching. The parties in Britain may be distinct from each other, but they are not very different from each other (1955: 52).

The ICPP data and our analyses might provide some insight into the "mirage" that the party responsibilists reported to have seen in Britain, and some notion of the options open to the American parties should they desire to provide more "choice." Table 3.3 provides the data necessary for the relevant comparisons on consistency, distance, and

TABLE 3.3   Comparative Data for United States and British Parties, 1957–62 Period

	Position[a]	Distance[b]	Consistency[c]
U.S. Democratic	−1.50 ⎱	3.50	−1.50
U.S. Republican	2.00 ⎰		− .50
U.K. Labour	−3.50 ⎱	2.75	− .75
U.K. Conservative	− .75 ⎰		−2.25

[a] The scores in this column are the mean positions taken by the parties on each of the four issue variables. A negative value means a "leftist" position, and a positive value means a "rightist" position. Because the "center" position on all four issues is 0, the magnitude (i.e., absolute value) of the parties' position scores can be taken as an indicator of "extremism." The actual position scores obtained by the parties in this study range from −5 to +4.

[b] The "distance" between parties is simply the difference of their mean issue positions. The actual values obtained by the party systems in this study range from 0 to +8.0.

[c] "Consistency" is measured as the negative of the average deviation of the individual issue positions from the mean party position. By this procedure, smaller negative scores (i.e., "higher" scores) indicate greater consistency (see note 5). The actual values obtained by the parties in this study range from 0 to −3.5.

ideological position. According to these data, then, what actually *were* the differences between the two systems for the 1957–1962 period?

First, what little difference exists on consistency of issue positions would seem to favor the American parties. Though the differences are so slight that they might easily be the products of measurement error, it is at least unlikely that the British parties hold the large edge that the APSA Report could have led us to expect. As for distance, here, too, a slight edge is given to the American parties. As Butler said, the British parties may have *appeared* to be further apart, but the looks were apparently deceiving.

The British system *did* differ from the American, though, in two ways, neither of which is insignificant in helping to clarify the choices for the British voters and both of which may help to explain the "mirage." Our comparison of the position scores reveals that the British Labour party was the sole British or American party that approximated "extreme." Where both American parties hovered near the middle of the scale, the British were offered a centrist and a moderately leftist party. This is one possible reason why the British parties appeared to provide a clearer choice.

Another likely factor is the greater cohesion of the British parties in their legislature. We have attempted a graphic comparison in Figure 3.4 to illustrate (and, undoubtedly, exaggerate) the point. The greatest inconsistency in the American case may be found not in the planks of a platform nor even in the positions taken by the party over time but rather in the behaviour of the party's legislators. When the British observe their legislators, they are provided with something resembling

FIGURE 3.4 Images Provided by Legislators' Behavior: Hypothetical Mean Voting Positions of Legislators in the U.S. and U.K.

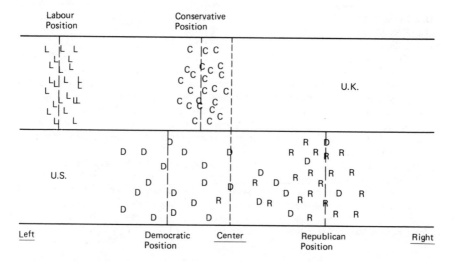

two distinct blocks; the Americans see two overlapping clouds. It is probably safe to conjecture that given two systems with all else equal, the one with the greater party cohesion will *appear* to provide more significant choices and in fact will provide its voters with greater clarity of choice.

What, then, can we say to those who would have the American parties provide clearer choices? We have seen from our analyses that ideological distance is profoundly affected by the environment within which the parties operate. Short of revising the environment, we might expect little in the way of the parties' actually *moving* apart. (And that would, in any case, go contrary to the ideological convergence that is being reported in the rest of the world today; see Thomas, 1975.) Though one or the other of the parties could begin to shift the entire system in one direction or the other to better approximate what was available in Britain in the 1957–62 period, there would appear to be little inclination on the part of either of the parties (or the voters) to leave the traditionally safe lane in the middle of the road.[10] According to our argument, that would seem to leave the option of strengthening the national parties in ways that would encourage greater party cohesion in Congress. Whether the parties *can* do so, especially given America's system of separation of powers, is left to Chapters 5 and 6; whether they *will* do so is left to speculation in Chapter 7. But for those who would make the American parties more responsible, clarifying the differences that already exist may at least provide an acceptable (and much more feasible) alternative to actually widening the gap. Clarifying party differences is basically a matter for party organization to develop and party cohesion to reflect. We turn to these matters in the next two chapters.

NOTES

1. Others, including Finlay et al. (1974), might disagree that the terms "left" and "right" are as applicable in the third World, but there is less disagreement about the applicability of the *concepts* to the third World setting. We should also note that the liberal/conservative conflict is still alive in some third World countries, where issues of rights and liberties are still hotly debated. Our own data for liberal/conservative issue show that this is the case (see Harmel, 1979a).

2. In recent years a literature has developed which argues that we are witnessing the "end of ideology." For a collection of articles on the subject, see Mostafa Rejai (ed.), *Decline of Ideology?* (Chicago: Aldine-Atherton, 1971).

3. Originally, each of the parties was assigned a value ranging from −5 to +5 for each of the issue variables, with negative numbers implying greater "rightism." For purposes of illustration, it proved useful here to reverse the signs, associating the negative signs with the "left" side of a visual display. This practice is followed throughout this study.

4. Our usage of the term "ideological distance" seems to be consistent with Sartori's (1976: 126), though his application is primarily to societies and ours is to parties. Our usage is identical to that of Monica Charlot (1975) in her longitudinal study of ideological distance in Britain.

5. Since the average deviation becomes larger as the consistency decreases, we actually use the negative of the average deviation as a measure of "consistency."

6. For some purposes, it might be preferable to consider the number of parties as a characteristic of the party system, rather than as a feature of the "environment." However, the theoretical arguments set forth here, whether referring to the ideological nature of an individual party or of the entire party system, are largely based on the electoral considerations of the individual parties. Therefore, since the number of parties is a feature of the context within which those considerations are made, we will consistently refer to "number of parties" as an environmental variable.

7. For the "electoral system" variable, proportional systems were assigned a value of "1" and plurality systems were assigned a value of "2."

8. Our measure of "coalition propensity" is based on data from Banks' (1971) Cross-Polity Time Series data set. The "electoral system" variable is based on Blondel's (1969) six-category variable. Of the six categories, two are clearly P.R. and three are clearly majority. Only the alternative-vote, two-ballot system could fit either category, but we have chosen to include such systems as P.R. based on Eckstein's argument (1963: 252) that these systems share important features relevant to the establishment and survival of minor parties. P.R. systems are coded "1" and plurality systems as "2," making the expected direction of relationships negative. The data for "sectoral inequality" (sectoral income GINI) and affluence (GNP/capita in 1960) are from *World Handbook II*. For five of the eight cases where the sectoral GINI is missing, it was possible to use the individual income GINI to estimate the sectoral measure by regression analysis. Because only 18 of our countries are included in the Sigelman and Yough (1978) study, it was necessary to recompute the "tolerance" variable for the 28 countries; "freedom of group opposition," one of their indicators of tolerance, does not vary over our sample.

Our choice of indicators for the independent variables has been influenced by Sigelman and Yough (1978) and by the relevant literature which they ably review. They also provide a concise summary of the arguments underlying the relationship of affluence to equality and to left-right "polarization." Much of the reasoning presented in their discussion of "Model I" on pages 358–359 also applies here.

9. Because these are country-level rather than party-level variables, the E^2 statistic discussed in Chapter 2 and employed in the next three chapters is not applicable here.

10. For information relevant to the argument that the 1980 elections may have signaled a dramatic "shift to the right," see Chapter 8 and especially notes 7, 8, and 9.

APPENDIX TO CHAPTER 3

The following are the codes assigned to the American parties for the issue variables discussed on pages 27–30 of Chapter 3. The codes and descriptions relate to the parties during the period 1957–62. (Codes are described on page 27).

Ownership of the Means of Production
Democrats: 1   Republicans: 3

In general, the Democrats did not advocate governmental control of basic industries, though they did favor government ownership of power facilities in the South and the West. Republicans consistently opposed such projects as TVA and in fact worked to restore power developments to private enterprise. The Republicans also supported free enterprise with respect to common carrier transportation.

Government Role in Economic Planning
Democrats: −3   Republicans: 2

The Democrats pursued price controls and price supports, as well as tax reforms and monetary policies which would combine economic growth with economic justice. The Republicans opposed economic planning in principle, though they favored the role of the Federal Reserve System in controlling the economy and credit.

Redistribution of the Wealth   Democrats: −1   Republicans: 2

The Democrats supported measures for progressive taxation, while the Republicans were somewhat more likely to Favor legislative programs that would give more favorable treatment to higher-income groups.

Providing for Social Welfare   Democrats: −3   Republicans: 1

The Democrats consistently favored a mixture of obligatory programs of public assistance and voluntary programs, though some Southern Democrats voted against such measures. The Republicans emphasized the individual's responsibility to care for himself but did favor the social security program.

---

* More detailed descriptions are provided in Janda (1980a); note that the coding values have been reversed from the original scheme, so that negative values here are on the "left" side of the ideological continuum.

4

The Environment and Party Organization

Political parties are commonly regarded as social organizations with political objectives. As organizations, parties involve recurring interactions among individuals based on a division of labor and role differentiation. The nature and extent of a party's organizational structure is thought to have consequences for its activities. Duverger, the foremost contemporary student of party organization, held that organization

> constitutes the general setting for the activity of members, the selection of leaders, and decides their powers. It often explains the strength and efficiency of certain parties, the weakness and inefficiency of others (1961: 4).

Moreover, it is the organizational aspect of political parties that gives them substance and identity apart from their prominent candidates and transient leaders. As Wilson notes, "Organization provides continuity and predictability to social processes that would otherwise be episodic and uncertain" (1973: 7). If parties are to be regarded as anything more than momentary alliances of candidates under the same label to appeal for votes in elections, it is due to their organization.

It is not surprising, then, that party organization has drawn the attention of party reformers. Proposals for making the American parties more "responsible" have commonly focused on restructuring the party organization. The APSA Report (Appendix A, p. 146) urged reducing the size of the national conventions but holding longer and more frequent meetings—once every two years rather than every presidential election year. The Report also proposed the creation of a "party council" for each party consisting of 50 members drawn from the national committee, the congressional party organizations, state committees, governors, and other high party officials—including the President. These councils would meet at least quarterly to make a preliminary draft of the party platform, interpret the platform in relation to current problems, make recommendations to appropriate party organs regarding congressional candidates, bring to the attention of the national convention or committee conspicuous departures of state or local party organizations from national party decisions, and even discuss and perhaps screen presidential candidates.

These proposals, which were never carried out, were in keeping with a desire to increase the importance of parties in government by improving their ability to coordinate individual actions and fix individual and group responsibility—in short, to improve the parties' organizational capacity. According to rational-efficient ideas of group action, increasing organizational capacity means developing more complex procedures for mobilizing and coordinating the efforts of party activists for executing party strategy and advancing party policies.

What is the feasibility of increasing the complexity of American party organization, given the physical, socioeconomic, and political environment in the United States? Our concern is not with the specific structure of any party but with the complexity of party organization in general.[1] Does cross-national analysis provide any evidence of environmental constraints on the complexity of the procedures for coordinating party actions?

MEASURING PARTY COMPLEXITY

The concept of party "complexity" subsumes the division of labor, formalization of rules, impersonality of relationships, and forms of role and structural differentiation.[2] In a nutshell, the more elaborate the party structure, the more *complex* it is. It should be noted that this dimension of party organization is distinctly different from the centralization of power within an organization, a concept studied in the next chapter. For now, it suffices to say that decentralization of power deals with the location of authority within the party, regardless of the complexity of its organization. Not only are the two concepts logically distinct, they are empirically unrelated.[3]

Party complexity is measured in our study by rating the parties on six different indicators:

1. **Structural articulation**—scored from 0 to 11, with higher scores awarded when numerous national organs have clear functional responsibilities.
2. **Intensiveness of organization**—scored from 1 to 6, with higher scores given when the organization is intense, i.e., the basic units are relatively small.

3. **Extensiveness of organization**—scored from 0 to 6, with higher scores assigned when the country is thoroughly covered with local units.
4. **Frequency of local meetings**—scored from 0 to 6, with higher scores assigned when local meetings are frequent.
5. **Maintaining records**—scored from 0 to 16, with higher scores given when the party has a publishing program, a research division, and accurate membership lists.
6. **Pervasiveness of organization**—scored from 0 to 18, with higher scores assigned when the party penetrates many socioeconomic sectors and claims many supporters within each sector.

The raw scores assigned to the Democratic and Republican parties on these indicators are reported in the appendix to this chapter. These scores and the scores for all other parties in the study were standardized to a common metric. Each party's standardized scores on the six variables were then averaged to form a composite score for that party.[4] High positive scores denote high degrees of party complexity, high negative scores denote low degrees, and average amounts of complexity hover around 0. For example, the lowest complexity score was −2.70 and was obtained by the Greek Liberal party. The highest score of 1.15 was earned by the German Social Democratic party. The average complexity score for all the parties was −.13. When we speak about variance in party complexity, we will be referring to variation in party scores on this scale.

ASSESSING ENVIRONMENTAL EFFECTS ON PARTY COMPLEXITY

That the environment does have an effect on party complexity is presumed by scholars who rate countries according to the organization of their parties.[5] They recognize organizational differences among parties in the same country but see them tending toward a modal type, displaying a "center of gravity" that usefully distinguishes countries (Pride, 1970: 698). Conventional wisdom, for example, holds that American parties tend to be weakly organized.[6] Sorauf bluntly states:

> Even by the standards of the parties of the other democracies, the American party organizations cut an unimpressive figure. . . . Instead of a continuity of relationships and of operations, the American party organization features only improvisatory, elusive, and sporadic structure and activities (1972: 133).

How much do parties in the same country "cluster" in organizational complexity, thereby reflecting the common impact of their environment, and how well do the American parties actually compare to parties in other countries? The effects of environment are portrayed in Figure 4.1.

FIGURE 4.1   Degree of Party Organization, by Country

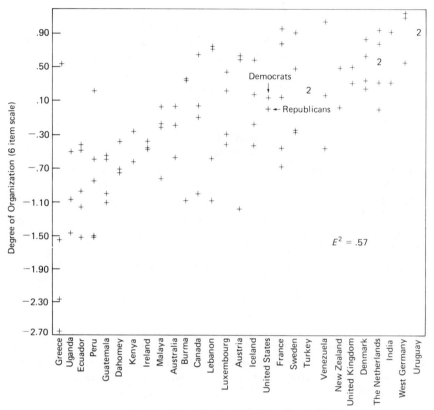

Countries Ordered by Increasing Party Organization

It is evident that the countries vary substantially in the "centers of gravity" of the party organizations and that parties within countries do tend to cluster together in complexity. The E^2 value of .57 reported in Figure 4.1 indicates that 57 percent of the variance in organizational complexity can be explained by the identity of the country, which suggests an upper limit for environmental effects on party complexity.

As for the American parties, they obtain very similar scores, with the Republicans slightly lower than the Democrats. Their average score (.08) is somewhat *higher* than the mean for all 95 competitive parties in the sample; this contradicts "conventional wisdom." Even with comparisons limited to only the European democracies, the average score for the Democrats and Republicans is exactly equal to the mean score on party organization of 42 European parties. It appears, then, that American parties are very similar in their degree of organization and are not lacking in complexity compared to other democratic parties.

Lest this assessment seem too deviant from the accepted understanding of American party organization, it is appropriate to recall the distinction between the complexity of organization, measured here, and the location of power within the organization, treated in the next chapter. Most characterizations of American parties as being "weakly" organized pertain to their decentralization of power rather than the complexity of their structure. When concern is limited to structural complexity, American parties *do* tend to possess as much organization as most other competitive parties.

The positions of some of those other parties on the organizational dimension (see Figure 4.1) are also worthy of note. As might be expected, the three German parties stand near the top of the list in organizational complexity, but surprisingly they are outranked by the two parties in Uruguay. Uruguay owes its high rank in party complexity to the peculiar nature of its Blanco and Colorado parties. Some say they are really *coalitions* of other parties that compete against one another in elections and apportion governmental positions according to their electoral success. Whether Uruguay should be considered a two-party or a highly fragmented, multiparty system has generated some discussion by Latin Americanists.[7] Because we have chosen to count it as a two-party system, the Blancos and Colorados obtain a high complexity score, for their factional components contribute greatly to their structural differentiation.

The placement of the other parties in the list should not raise as many eyebrows. The Western European parties tend to score near the top (except for the Greek parties, which are commonly characterized as low in organization, see Legg, 1968: 438–439), and parties in Third World countries that qualified as democracies during our time period tend to rank below average. As the data indicate, one can do fairly well in predicting a party's organizational complexity simply by knowing its country identity—and then consulting this listing.

EXPLAINING ENVIRONMENTAL EFFECTS ON COMPLEXITY

Although organizational complexity can be "explained" in large part by country identity, this is an unsatisfying explanation. As argued in Chapter 1, it is an idiographic rather than a nomothetic explanation. We must also seek to understand what factors in the countries' environments account for varying levels of organizational complexity. It is then possible to judge the success of this search for explanation by seeing how much of the country-specific variance (57 percent) we can recapture with theoretical explanations for environmental effects. The search begins by identifying individual explanatory factors that have been proposed as causes of party complexity.

Individual Explanatory Factors

Our search for theoretical explanations of organizational complexity leads first to the literature on organizational theory and two social factors, modernity and population size. Then we will examine four political factors that are often mentioned as causes of party complexity: the electoral system, the breadth of the franchise, the age of democratic institutions, and the extent of party competition.

Social scientists have cited such aspects of *modernity* as urbanization, high literacy, and social wealth as conducive to the formation of complex organizations. In more general terms, Stinchcombe (1965) has proposed that "modern" societies are more likely than "traditional" ones to provide conditions for forming organizations and allowing them to flourish. Stinchcombe suggests several indicators of modernity; we use his notion of a money economy, which we measure by the proportion of wage and salary earners in the labor force. The higher the proportion of workers receiving monetary payments, the more modern the socioeconomic environment and the more conducive it should be to the emergence of rational-efficient social organizations.

Other scholars have proposed that the complexity of organizations tends to reflect the *complexity of their environment*. Hall (1977: 151), for instance, has suggested that an organization becomes structurally differentiated to deal with the scope and diversity of its environment. For our study, the complexity of the environment is measured simply by the size of the population. The larger the country's population, the greater the complexity of its national organizations, including its parties.[8]

The influence of the *electoral system* on party organization has been emphasized in Duverger's writings (1963 and 1964). Duverger contended that voting for lists of candidates in proportional representation arrangements (as in The Netherlands) promotes party organization, while voting for individual candidates in single-member districts with simple plurality vote (as in the United States) weakens it. Using a second ballot to decide elections when no candidate has a majority (as in France) has a mixed effect. Because this theory requires more refined measurement of electoral systems than the dichotomy of plurality versus proportional systems used in Chapter 3, we employ the full scale developed by Blondel (1969: 534). This allows us to accommodate Duverger's classification of electoral systems while incorporating arguments that multi-member districts demand more party organization than single-member districts. At the low end of the scale is proportional representation with all members of the parliament elected at large. At the other end is the single-member majority system with all members also elected at large. Single-member districts with single and second-ballot systems are placed in the middle.[9] With the "electoral system" variable coded in this manner, we expect an inverse relationship between the electoral system scale and party complexity. Parties that exist in countries at the proportional representation (low) end of the scale should score higher in complexity than those in countries with single-member districts at the upper end.

Another electoral variable, the *"breadth of the franchise"*, has been offered as a political factor affecting party complexity. Rokkan (1970: Chapts. 3 and 7), for instance, has argued that parties develop more complex organizations to attract voting support when the electorate is larger. We have coded the countries into one of two categories for this variable. Universal adult suffrage (with varying definitions of "adult") is the broadest condition of suffrage in our sample, and it existed in 23 countries during our time period. Literacy requirements restricted the franchise most often in the other five countries.[10] The broader the franchise, the greater should be the party complexity.

The *age of democratic institutions* is another political factor thought to affect party organization. It is posited that party organization takes time to develop and that countries with long histories of democratic institutions have provided more time for parties to build complex organizations. Unfortunately, there is no easy way to date the onset of democracy, for different dates are found for the establishment of the secret ballot and the creation of parliaments that are responsible to the public. Following Hewitt (1977), we measure the "democratic experience" according to the dates for universal male suffrage, the secret ballot, and responsible government, but we take the *average* of these three dates in years as our variable. The more recent the introduction of democratic institutions, the less complex the party organization is expected to be.

The last political factor to be considered here is the *degree of party competition* within the system. Highly competitive systems are likely to feature parties that are well organized to contest elections. Where one party consistently dominates, organization may be unnecessary for the victorious party and pointless for the other(s). Several scholars have studied the relationship between party competition and party organization in the United States, and most have found a positive relationship.[11] For example, Crotty's study of North Carolina found "a decided affinity between the strength of the local party organization as measured by the Party Organization Scale and the closeness of electoral contests in a county" (1967: 258). Party competition is less frequently cited as contributing to party organization in the cross-national literature. Perhaps this is due to the ease of measuring competition in the simple two-party case and the difficulty of measuring it across systems varying from two to six parties. Our measure adjusts for the number of parties and expresses the spread in proportions of votes won by all parties in the country as a *lack* of party competition.[12] The larger the vote spread among parties in the same country, the less competitive the party system and the less complex its parties should be.

Modernity, population size, nature of the electoral system, breadth of franchise, length of experience with democracy, and degree of party competition have all been suggested as environmental factors influencing the complexity of party organization. Table 4.1 reports the simple correlations of each of these variables with the scale of party complexity. Although every factor is correlated with party complexity in the hypothesized direction, none of the correlations are especially large and one is statistically insignificant. Among these six factors, the strongest single explanation of environmental effects is "modernity," or the proportion of the labor force paid wages and salaries, which explains only 21 percent of the variance. We have noted in the previous section that the identity of a country (i.e., its environment) can explain 57 percent of the variance in party complexity cross-nationally. Judged against that standard, none of these factors, when taken individually, constitute an adequate explanation of the environmental effects we have observed. Each explanation is inadequate because no single cause captures the multiplicity of causes represented by the "environment." To reflect environmental effects more accurately, we must, at the very least, employ all six factors *simultaneously* in explaining party complexity.

TABLE 4.1   Bivariate Correlations between Environmental Variables and Party Complexity

Environmental Factor	Simple Correlation r	Explained Variance[a] r^2
Modernity	.46*	.21
Population (log)	.16	.03
Electoral system	−.38*	.14
Restrictions on suffrage	−.39*	.15
Recency of democratic experience	−.28*	.08
Lack of party competition	−.19*	.04

[a] The variance in complexity explained by each environmental factor is computed by squaring the simple correlation.
* Correlation is significant at .05 level.

Explanatory Factors Combined

The multiple regression model created from the six environmental factors is presented in Table 4.2. The squared multiple correlation coefficient is .44, signifying that 44 percent of the variance in party complexity can be explained by the joint effect of these environmental variables.

While this may not be impressive when judged against 100 percent as the standard of complete explanation, it may seem more of an achievement when compared to the overall estimate of environmental effects, i.e., the E^2 of 57 percent. Thus the six variables actually explain 77 percent (44 divided by 57) of the variance available for explanation with environmental factors. Given the relatively large amount of error in measuring social science data (including party complexity), our model appears to be quite satisfactory in capturing the country effects with only six environmental variables.

TABLE 4.2 Multiple Regression for Party Complexity with Environmental Variables

Environmental Factor	Standardized Regression Coefficient[a]
Modernity	.56*
Population	.32*
Electoral system	−.30*
Restrictions on suffrage	−.21*
Recency of democratic experience	.37*
Lack of party competition	−.19*
R^2 = .44 Adjusted R^2 = .40 N = 95	

[a] Only the standardized regression coefficients are given because of the arbitrary scaling employed for some variables.
* Significant at the .05 level.

Table 4.2 reveals that all six factors in the equation are statistically significant. This includes population size, which fell short of significance for the simple correlation. Not only did incorporating these variables in a multivariate model fail to "wash out" any predicted relationships, but the general tendency was actually to enhance the influence of each factor when the other factors were held constant. Like the *ceteris paribus* condition in economic theory, when other things are equal (or held constant) and not allowed to confound the analysis, the effect of each environmental factor on party complexity is seen more clearly.

But Table 4.2 also reveals one notable reversal of sign from the original prediction. Although recency of democratic experience was found to be negatively related to party complexity in the simple correlation, the sign of the coefficient for recency of democratic experience in Table 4.2 is *positive*, indicating that parties in countries with younger institutions are *more* complex rather than less.[13]

This apparent anomaly conflicts with the theory that experience with democratic institutions increases party organization, but propositions in both organizational theory and party theory can accommodate the apparent discrepancy. For example, Stinchcombe (1965: 154) contends that organizations are formed according to the socially possible forms available at the time, while Evan (1976: 144) holds that the climate of an organization tends to be perpetuated from one generation of members to another.

Relatedly, Duverger (1961: 22–37) made a distinction between archaic party organization, formed around groups of notables in nineteenth-century politics, and modern party structure, directed toward organizing as large a proportion of the masses as possible. Because these newer forms of parties tended to be associated with "leftist" parties, Duverger spoke of a process of "contagion" from the left to describe the non-leftist parties' efforts to develop their party organization in response to the success of leftist parties within the same countries. Our data support Duverger's argument. In countries with old and successful leftist parties, the *non*-leftist parties are more likely to be highly organized than those in countries without leftist parties or with ones which are either young or electorally weak ($r = .30$).[14]

In short, countries which were late in developing democratic institutions tend to produce parties which are organizationally more complex than those which were founded in early democracies. This may be due to the more leftist orientations of newer parties, to the conscious copying of modern party structure,[15] or to the rational choice of the most effective form of organization necessary to win votes, given contemporary technological and social developments (Aldrich and Pfeffer, 1976). Whatever the specific reason, the recency of democratic experience does not show this relationship with party complexity in a simple correlation because of the confounding influence of modernity, which is correlated to democratic experience at the very high level of $-.77$. Because modern countries have had earlier democratic experiences, the separate effects of each variable emerge only when the other variable is controlled in the multivariate analysis.

With this reformulation of the theoretical argument, the multiple-factor explanation can be regarded as a relatively successful attempt to capture the environmental effects on party complexity with only six variables. A graphic demonstration of that success is given in Figure 4.2, which plots the party complexity scores for all 95 parties against the predicted degree of organization as calculated by the six-factor regression equation. The scores for all parties in a given country are plotted above the same point on the baseline, since the parties in each country receive the same *predicted* value for complexity because they share their country's environmental characteristics.[16]

Some countries (e.g., Greece, Guatemala, Uganda, and the United States) possess parties that are lower in organizational complexity than predicted by the environmental factors in our equation, while other countries (e.g., New Zealand and India) have parties that are more complex than predicted by the equation. No doubt there are additional

FIGURE 4.2   Environmental Effects on Party Organization

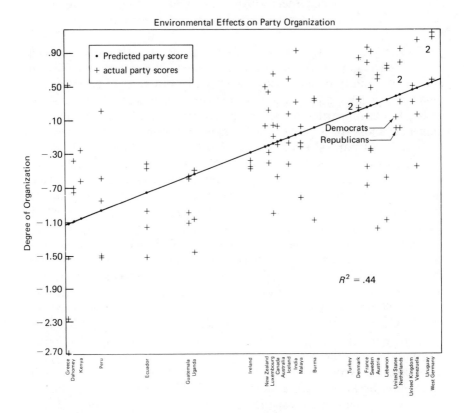

aspects of the country environment that could explain some of these deviations. Nevertheless, the six variables considered here can account for
most of the environmental effects on party complexity.

ANALYZING THE AMERICAN PARTIES

This inquiry into environmental effects on the organizational complexity
of political parties originated with an interest in determining the prospects of success for those who would make American parties more "responsible" for their actions in government. Proposals to increase party
responsibility have usually been linked to recommendations for restructuring the parties' organization to improve their policy-making capacity
and legislative cohesion.

The APSA recommendations of 1950 were questioned for their desirability as well as their feasibility, and they were not carried out. The
recent reform movement within the Democratic party, however, resulted
in a new party charter, adopted in 1974, which elaborated the organiza-

tion far beyond its previous state. The Charter is reprinted here as Appendix B. The Democratic National Committee was increased to 350 members (Article Three), the Executive Committee was reconstituted by providing for half the delegates to be selected by regional caucuses of National Committee members (Article Four, Section 2), and new organs were established in the form of a Judicial Council (Article Seven), a National Finance Council (Article Eight), and a National Education and Training Council (Article Nine). Although the new structure has been enshrined in paper, there is some doubt about its actual operations, particularly the roles being performed by the Judicial Council and the Education and Training Council (see Crotty, 1978: 250).

The 1950 APSA proposal for more responsible parties was criticized in part because it proposed a type of party organization that was not "suitable" for the United States. Hence, it is appropriate to wonder whether the Democrats have developed their organization beyond the hospitality of the American environment. And that brings us to the question: Does the United States environment impose limits on attempts to change the organizational character of American parties?

The evidence from the cross-national analysis suggests that environmental factors, accounting for 57 percent of the variance observed among 95 parties in 28 countries, do indeed impose strong constraints on party complexity. The most complex parties are found in countries with (1) a modern economy, (2) a large population, (3) broad suffrage, (4) close party competition, (5) proportional representational electoral systems, and (6) little experience with democratic institutions. The United States possesses all but the last two of these characteristics, and indeed its parties rank somewhat above the mean already in organizational complexity. Because both the Republicans and the Democrats fall somewhat below their "predicted" position according to the six environmental factors, one might expect that there is still some "room" for increasing their complexity within the limits of environmental constraints. At least it seems clear that the United States parties were not already straining beyond their environmental limitations as of 1957–1962. Despite the many changes in our environment since then, changes which might further limit organizational complexity have not occurred on our six environmental variables. Thus the data analysis for the earlier period seems to have relevance today. There is still some room for the parties to develop their organizational structure.

Party reformers of all dispositions have proposed changes in party structure. Those who wish to develop more responsible parties have often recommended the formation of more specialized party organs. The underlying assumption is that some degree of organizational elaboration is a prerequisite for strong, "responsible" parties. In other words, the objective has not been to increase organizational complexity per se, but to do so in order to make party organization more effective—to produce parties that are organized to enact their campaign promises into law upon winning control of the government. But while well-defined organization may be a necessary condition for strong parties, it would hardly be considered sufficient. At the very least, strong parties require an assemblage of power along with complex organization at the national level. Although the American parties have been shown to be moderately complex already, their national organizations are markedly lacking in power. We now turn to a more general discussion of that condition and an attempt to understand it.

NOTES

1. There are other dimensions to party organization. The conceptual framework of the ICPP project (Janda, 1980a) provides for analyzing parties according to their centralization of power, involvement of party members, coherence (factionalism), and autonomy from other sectors of society. The next chapter will focus on the decentralization of power within the parties. The two concepts, "organizational complexity" and "decentralization of power," are the most important in the *structure* of party organization.

2. Heydebrand's collection of empirical research on organizations classifies our concerns under the heading of "internal structural differentiation." When organizations are highly differentiated, they are viewed as bureaucracies. Perrow sees all large, complex organizations as bureaucracies, although in different degrees. See Heydebrand (1973), pp. 21–22, and Perrow (1972), Chap. 1.

Hall employs the term "complexity," but he distinguishes it from "formalization." See Hall (1977), Chaps. 5 and 6. Our usage of "complexity" conforms more directly to the "conformation" dimension of Eckstein and Gurr's (1975: 108–109) authority patterns.

3. The correlation between our measure of organizational complexity and decentralization of power is − .07 for the sample of 95 competitive parties analyzed in this study.

4. The scores for each variable were standardized by subtracting the variable's mean from the party scores and dividing the difference by the standard deviation of the party scores. Since the separate indicators are scored on different scales (i.e., the highest score for pervasiveness of organization is 18 while the highest score for extensiveness of organization is only 6), simply averaging the original, non-standardized scores might result in giving greater "weight" to one indicator than to another. Standardizing the scores before averaging them results in equal weighting for all variables in the composite score. The scale produced from the average standard scores (normally called "summated z-scores") had a reliability of .82, as computed by Conbach's alpha. See Janda (1980a), Chap. 14. The code categories are given in Janda (1980a) and in Janda (1979a). For a discussion of issues involved in the use of summated z-scoring, see Harmel (1981), note 3.

5. For example, the United States is said to have weak and decentralized parties, Britain is characterized as having strong and highly structured parties, and Latin American countries, in general, are thought to have little in the way

of party structure but to have strong personal leadership of party activities: See William Keefe, *Parties, Politics, and Public Policy in America, 2d Ed.* (1976), p. 29; Leon D. Epstein (1967b), p. 132; and Ronald H. McDonald (1971), p. 13.

6. Some of this conventional wisdom is summarized in Kenneth Janda (1980b).

7. See McDonald (1971), pp. 204–205, and Donald W. Bray, "Uruguay," in Ben G. Burnett and Kenneth F. Johnson (eds.), *Political Forces in Latin America* (Belmont, Calif.: Wadsworth, 1968), pp. 438–439.

8. To deal with the skewed distribution of countries by population, we actually use the logarithm of population size in this analysis.

9. The numbers of countries and parties at each point on Blondel's scale are as follows:

Countries	Code	Type of electoral system	Parties
2	1	Full P.R., whole country is constituency	10
12	2	P.R. within multi-member constituencies	41
2	3	Second ballot, single-member districts	8
9	4	Majority vote, single-member districts	24
2	5	Majority vote, multi-member districts	9
1	6	Majority vote, whole country constituency	3

Blondel reported data for only 24 of the 28 countries; the other 4 were coded using his criteria. In the correlational analysis, codes 5 and 6 were combined.

10. The countries with literacy restrictions on suffrage during our time period were Ecuador, Peru, Guatemala, Kenya, and Uganda.

11. See Paul Allen Beck, "Environment and Party: The Impact of Political and Demographic Country Characteristics on Party Behavior," *American Political Science Review*, Vol. 68 (September, 1974), pp. 1229–1244, for a review of this literature. Beck's own research involving data on party chairmen in 129 counties during the 1964 election produced mixed results, with competitiveness tending to result in greater organization for Republicans but not for Democrats.

12. The number of parties in the system is determined by the criteria for inclusion in the ICPP project (Janda, 1980a), which require that parties win at least 5 percent of the seats in the legislature in two elections during our time period. In practice, this eliminates the minor parties in fragmented systems, leaving only the "most important" parties. Our measure of the lack of party competition adjusts for voting strength by multiplying the average proportion of votes won by a party by the number of parties in the system. This adjustment gives more credit for a party's winning 50 percent of the votes in a three-party than in a two-party system, for example. The lack of party competition is measured then by computing the standard deviation of the adjusted voting strength over all the parties in the system. The larger the standard deviation, the less the party competition.

13. Removing the recency of democratic experience from the equation does not "solve" the problem. The remaining five variables explain only 39 percent of the variance. Moreover, removing recency of democratic experience depresses almost all the remaining coefficients, especially that of the proportion paid wages and salaries, which falls from .56 to .27. This occurs *despite* the correlation of −.77 between recency of democratic experience and proportion paid wages and salaries. This means that after "modernity" has been controlled, countries with more recently developed democratic institutions tend to have more complex parties than countries with longer experience with universal suffrage, secret ballot, and responsible government. This phenomenon is seen most clearly in the United States and Greece, both of which are predicted to have more organized parties without allowing for the recency of democratic experience in the equation.

14. Our measure of the "leftist threat" to non-leftist parties in a country is computed by multiplying the proportion of votes won by leftist parties (either Communist or non-Communist left as classified by the Bureau of Intelligence and Research, U.S. Department of State, in *World Strength of the Communist Party Organizations*) by the party's age, under the assumption that both electoral success and permanence are necessary to induce non-leftist parties to organize in response to electoral challenges from leftist parties. This measure is then correlated with the complexity shown by the 66 remaining *non*-leftist parties.

15. For a general discussion of cultural contagion which has bearing on the copying of party structure, see Marc Howard Ross and Elizabeth Homer (1976).

16. Of course, differences among parties within a country can be attributed to other differing characteristics of the individual parties (see Figure 2.1).

APPENDIX TO CHAPTER 4

The following are the codes assigned to the American parties for the organization variables discussed on pages 43 and 44 of Chapter 4. The codes and descriptions relate to the parties during the period 1957–62. (Codes are described on pages 43 and 44.)

Structural Articulation   Democrats: 10   Republicans: 10

Each party maintained four major organizational components (national convention, national committee, and House and Senate campaign committees). Procedures for selecting the party leaders were quite clearly specified, though the functional responsibilities of the four components were ambiguous.

Intensiveness of Organization   Democrats: 5   Republicans: 5

Both parties were organized mainly on the basis of precincts, which typically encompassed 1000 or fewer voters.

Extensiveness of Organization   Democrats: 6   Republicans: 5

The Democrats maintained precinct organizations virtually throughout the country. Because Republican organization was sparse in the South, the Republican party receives a slightly lower score.

Frequency of Local Meetings   Democrats: 2   Republicans: 2

Local party organizations were likely to meet only at campaign times.

Maintaining Records   Democrats: 9   Republicans: 12

While both parties maintained a publishing program and research divisions, both activities were more active within the Republican party. Both parties maintained mailing lists for fund-raising purposes, but they were not "membership lists" per se.

Pervasiveness of Organization   Democrats: 7   Republicans: 3

The Republican party's allied organizations included women's and youth groups, as did the Democratic party's. The Democrats also held close association with labor organizations at both state and national levels.

* More detailed descriptions are provided in Janda (1980s). The values provided here are the original values assigned to the parties. The scores represented in Figures 4.1 and 4.2 are composite standardized scores; see page 44 and note 4 on page 54.

5

The Environment and Decentralization of Party Power

INTRODUCTION

If the authors of the APSA Report argued for more organization and ideological clarity in the American party system, they were *emphatic* about the need for strengthening the American national party organizations relative to their state and local counterparts: local party organizations should show "loyalty" to the whole organization, and national organizations should "deal with" disloyal state organizations. (See Appendix A, p. 146.) How, the authors wondered, could the American parties put forth coherent programs, require their elected officials to support those programs, and ultimately provide the voters with a vision of unified, well-organized parties, if the national parties lacked the power to control either their state and local namesakes or even their own national business?

The *fact* that the American parties were, and are, decentralized has found little disagreement among students of those parties. Recently, Keefe has asserted that:

> There is no lively debate among political scientists concerning the dominant characteristic of American political parties. It is, pure and simple, their decentralization (1972: 25).

And thirty years earlier, Schattschneider had indicated the importance that students of American parties attributed and would continue to attribute to this particular characteristic of the parties:

> Decentralization of power is by all odds the most important single characteristic of the American major party; more than anything else this trait distinguishes it from all others. Indeed, *once this truth is understood, nearly everything else about American parties is greatly illuminated* (1942: 129; emphasis added).

But while it has been widely accepted that the American parties *are* decentralized, there is less agreement with the Report's assertion that they *could be* less so. Given the environment within which the parties must operate, the critics have argued, could the American parties centralize, even if they wanted to, and still remain viable political entities? Or put another way: Are parties' structures so constrained by forces external to the parties that internal reform efforts may be irrelevant at best or at worst disastrous?

The APSA Committee clearly felt that more party centralization could be achieved as an internal party affair, without changing the constitutional system within which the parties operate. The Report did recognize the decentralization of the American government (as formalized in its federal structure) and the presidential system with its separation of powers as hindrances to party centralization, but *not* insurmountable hindrances. So instead of suggesting constitutional change, the Committee proposed a number of structural changes within the parties themselves. (See Appendix A, Part II.) As Kirkpatrick puts it in his later review of the Report and related literature, the Committee's proposals were based on the assumption that:

> Naturally, some restructuring of national party organizations would be required to provide strong, representative, policy-oriented leadership. It would be essential to reform the existing relations between state and local parties, on the one hand, and national parties on the other (1971: 968).

The charge to the parties was clear: *Change thyselves!*

But considerable doubt is raised about parties' abilities to change *themselves* by Epstein (1967a) and Keefe (1972). Keefe's assertion that "the parties are less what they make of themselves than what their environment makes of them" has echoed through much of the recent literature on the American parties. If such factors as large country size, heterogeneity of the society, sectionalism, and the federal system have led to the decentralization of the American parties, then what likelihood of success should be attributed to a party's unilateral attempts to alter its structure? To the extent that our empirical investigations suggest a prominent role for the environment, doubt must be raised about a totally internal assault on party decentralization.

MEASUREMENT OF PARTY DECENTRALIZATION

As we are using the term here, "decentralization of power" refers to the distribution of control over decision making among the levels of party organization. In particular, the concept involves the extent to which the national level of party organization is free from control by the regional and the local levels in conducting what would normally be considered national party business and is capable of enforcing its decisions on the subnational organs.[1]

In listing the areas of party business which are most important to winning governmental office and conducting the party's other ongoing business, one would certainly include (1) involvement in communications media, (2) administration of party discipline, (3) selection of candidates for the national legislature, (4) allocation of funds, (5) selection of party leadership, and (6) formulation of party policy. These six areas of party decision making underlie our measurement of decentralization, with another indicator added to tap the more general, structural embodiment of decentralization. The seven measures used for rating the parties on this concept are:

1. **Control over communications**—scored from 0 to 7, with low scores given to parties where the national (rather than regional or local) level of organization controls important party media.

2. **Administration of discipline**—scored from 0 to 4, with low scores given to parties where a national organ administers discipline over party members.

3. **Selection of legislative candidates**—scored from 1 to 9, with low scores given to parties where selection is done by a national organ.

4. **Allocation of funds**—scored from 0 to 6, with low scores given to parties where party funds are collected and allocated primarily by the national level.

5. **Selection of national party leader**—scored from 0 to 8, with low scores given to parties with selection by a national party organ.

6. **Formulation of party policy**—scored from 0 to 7, with low scores given to parties where policies are formulated by a national organ.

7. **Nationalization of structure**—scored from 0 to 6, with low scores given to parties where there is a hierarchical structure with the national level in ultimate control.

The scores on these measures were standardized and combined to yield a single, composite score for decentralization. Because national control received the low scores on each of these measures, high overall scores indicate a higher degree of decentralization of power; low scores indicate centralization.

ASSESSING ENVIRONMENTAL EFFECTS ON PARTY DECENTRALIZATION

We have already noted that Keefe and other students of the American parties have considered the United States environment to be conducive

FIGURE 5.1 Countries Ordered by Increasing Party Decentralization

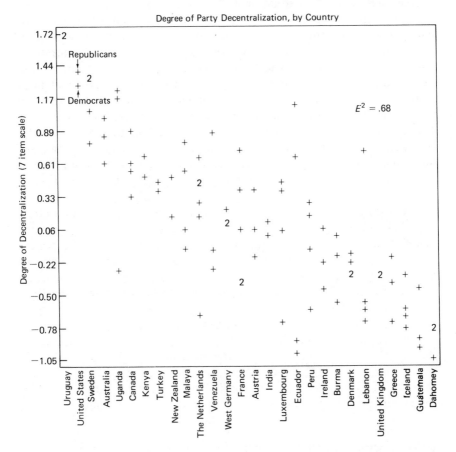

Degree of Party Decentralization, by Country

to decentralized structures for both the Democratic and the Republican parties. Blondel has generalized the influence of the environment to parties of other systems in arguing that "in all cases, the influence of outside elements has played a part in the development of modification of internal [party] structures..." (1969: 125). Figure 5.1 does indeed indicate a high degree of similarity among the structures of a given country's parties, when the full range of decentralization scores is taken into account. Fully 68 percent of the cross-national variation in decentralization can be explained by the country environment.

Among the most centralized parties (i.e., the least decentralized) are those of Dahomey and Guatemala, whose parties feature a high degree of "personalism," or devotion to the party leader. Among the most decentralized parties are the two in Uruguay and the two in the United States. We have already noted (in Chapter 4) the special circumstances of Uruguayan politics which have contributed to highly complex parties;

those same features have undoubtedly contributed to their decentralization as well. The "coalitional" nature of the Blanco and Colorado parties, owed in part to an electoral system that determines the victors of national office by summing the votes of factions which are separately identified on the ballot, is wholly consistent with a lack of centralized control generally. And Payne (1968) has suggested another contributing factor: the "status" orientation of Uruguayan presidential candidates leads them to emphasize personal electoral goals almost to the exclusion of organizational goals for the parties.[2] Though centralized control might be a value for the *party*, it could actually hurt the chances of the presidential candidate by alienating some of the factions whose votes are accumulated in the national candidate's total. Hence, centralized control is not only unnecessary but is actually unwanted by the national party leaders.

As for the American parties, their places among the most decentralized half-dozen parties in the sample support the claims of Keefe, Schattschneider, and others, that a distinguishing feature of the American parties is their degree of decentralization. Also not surprising are the more centralized positions of the British parties, sitting in marked contrast to their American counterparts. For those who saw in the British parties a higher degree of national control, and wanted that structure transported here, we can report that at least the empirical comparison was an accurate one. As for the feasibility of such a move, the E^2 of .68 suggests a large role for the environment in shaping its parties' structures; after considering some of the specific sources of environmental influence, we will be in a better position to suggest the extent to which the American environment *requires* such decentralized parties.

EXPLAINING ENVIRONMENTAL EFFECTS ON PARTY DECENTRALIZATION

The list of elements of the environment which could potentially have an influence on party structure is, of course, as long as the list of elements in that environment. However, the literature suggests a much smaller number of variables that stand out as the most theoretically important. We will discuss each of those variables individually first and then assess their combined explanatory value.

Individual Explanatory Factors

Preeminent among the suggested causes of decentralization, whether governmental or party, is the *size of the country* within which each operates. Blondel argues that "for polities as for other organizations,... the greater the distance between the centre and periphery, the more central-ized rule is to be avoided" (1969: 285). The sheer impracticality of trying to be the eyes and ears to the entire dispersed population has often become a burden for which both the leaders and the citizens of large nations have welcomed more localized governmental bodies with the power and the responsibility to make decisions on local issues. Like-wise, political parties may conclude that local party organs are better suited than the national level to making decisions concerning local issues and localized party activities. And in order to fulfill a function as a ma-jor conduit for political participation, parties in large countries may also be compelled to provide effective local organs for the convenience of those who wish to affect even the national party's business. Though these arguments do not imply the need for centralized parties in small countries, they do suggest that such parties have fewer reasons for de-centralization than the parties of large countries. In our analyses, the size of the country will be represented by the logarithm of its area in square kilometers.[3]

Along with the size of the country, the *social heterogeneity* of its population is often seen as a factor in party structure. If the party per-ceives a need to aggregate two or more socially diverse and sometimes politically inconsistent groups into the party fold, decentralization may be one means to that end. A decentralized structure may distribute deci-sion-making authority to levels of party organization that can more ade-quately respond to diverse interests in varied ways. This may be espe-cially valuable when the diversity is regional, i.e., when *sectionalism* is politically relevant. Hence, the sectional differences of the United States and Canada have often been cited as factors in those countries' decen-tralized parties. In the case of the United States, it has long been thought that the need to let Southern Democrats play to their own audi-ence in order to win elections has contributed to the party's willingness simply to close its eyes when the national platform is ignored. For our study, a measure of ethno-linguistic "fractionalization" serves as the in-dicator of social heterogeneity, and a separate "sectionalism" variable distinguishes among countries that are extremely, moderately, and neg-ligibly affected by sectional differences.[4]

Americanists often point to the system of *separation of powers* as another factor in the decentralization of the Democratic and Republican parties. Keefe, for instance, has argued that:

> One of the frequent by-products of this system is the emergence of a trun-cated party majority—that is, a condition under which one party controls one or both houses of the legislature and the other party controls the execu-tive. . . . at no time does [this] contribute a particle to the development and maintenance of party responsibility for a program of public policy (1980: 30–31).

And Madron and Chelf have noted that:

> "Since elected public officials belonging to the same party run largely inde-
> pendently of one another (from different geographical units, hence with dif-
> fering constituencies), they frequently feel their first obligation is to the
> constituency that elected them rather than to the party organization (or
> even the broader public interests of state or national policy-making)" (1974:
> 31).

One major component of the "separation of powers" formula, American style, is the separate selection of the president and the legislature,
in marked contrast to the more unified parliamentary system. In a parliamentary system, where the party's success is measured and rewarded
electorally as a unit, there is both a need for and a willingness to accept
central party direction. But in a presidential system, where legislators
and executives are rewarded separately in elections, control by the "center" (i.e., national party) is not only less necessary but actually may be
discouraged by a system of separation of powers.

However, presidentialism alone does not guarantee separation of
powers, and hence need not always result in decentralized parties. In
addition to the formal structure of the government, "separation of powers" also assumes that the legislature is an effective body in its own right
rather than merely a rubber stamp for the executive. Where the legislature is ineffective, especially in a formally presidential system (but in a
parliamentary system also), it is reasonable to expect that all of a major
party's tools will be used to acquire the executive office for the party's
candidate, with few resources and little power allocated to legislative
contests or lower party organs. Hence, we would expect the most decentralized parties to develop in presidential systems with effectively separated powers, with more centralized parties arising in parliamentary systems, and perhaps the *most* centralized parties in presidential systems
where the executive is dominant. We will use a set of "dummy" variables to stand for the four major types of horizontal governmental structures, as displayed in Figure 5.2.[5]

Finally, there seems to be little disagreement among those who have
written about political parties, either American or comparative, that
party structure tends to reflect the *vertical structure of the political system*. Lawson, for instance, notes that "decentralized, federal governments breed decentralized parties; centralized, unitary governments fos-
ter parties with power equally concentrated" (1976: 79). David Truman
has provided a concise version of the argument that usually underlies
such claims:

> The basic fact of federalism is that it creates self-sustaining centers of pow-
> er, privilege and profit which may be sought and defended as desirable in
> themselves, as means of leverage upon elements in the political structure
> above and below, and as bases from which individuals may move into

places of greater influence and prestige in and out of government (1955: 123).

But it is the very fact that federalism, per se, does not always guarantee "self-sustaining centers of power" which underscores the need for conceptual clarity when dealing with notions like "federalism" and "decentralization of power." To that end, we prefer to deal with governmental decentralization as two separate but related concepts, each of which taps a different dimension of the vertical decentralization of the polity. These concepts distinguish between formal, constitutional federalism and actual, effective distribution of power among the levels of government. The term "federalism" is here used to distinguish between those polities which have a formal federal structure and those that, at least on paper, are "unitary." A polity does not have to display actual decentralization of power in order to be a formally federal system; witness the "federal" but also centralized Soviet Union (and in our sample, Burma or Austria). "Decentralization of power," on the other hand, refers to the extent to which ultimate control (or ultimate policy making) is actually distributed among the levels of government. It would be theoretically possible for a polity to be formally unitary while maintaining an actual decentralization of power.

FIGURE 5.2*   Horizontal Governmental Structures

	Presidential Structure	Parliamentary Structure
Completely Effective Legislature	Separation of Powers (e.g., United States)	Effective Parliamentary (e.g., Britain)
Less than Effective Legislature	Strong Presidential (e.g., Ecuador)	Weak Parliamentary (e.g., Lebanon)

* The examples reflect the situations in those countries during the 1957–62 period of our data.

Since polities showing effective "decentralization of power" actually do create "self-sustaining centers of power, privilege and profit which may be sought and defended," we might expect the parties in such systems to develop decentralized structures so that party organs at the subnational levels will have sufficient leeway to effectively seek those centers, and that at least the leaders of the more localized organs will have some voice in national party affairs. Formally federal polities also offer at least the expectation of "self-sustaining centers of power," though that expectation is not always consistent with reality; hence we expect a lesser relationship between the presence of constitutional federalism and party decentralization. In the following analyses, two dichotomous variables distinguish between (1) formally federal and formally unitary systems and (2) effectively decentralized and effectively centralized polities.[6]

So in the following analyses, areal size, social heterogeneity, and sectionalism represent the physical and social dimension of the party's environment. The polity's vertical distribution of power, both formally and effectively, and the horizontal structure of the national government reflect the nature of the political system. After assessing the bivariate association of party decentralization with each of the environmental variables, we will combine them in multivariate analysis in order to assess their aggregate explanatory power.

TABLE 5.1 Bivariate Correlations between Environmental Variables and Party Decentralization[a]

Environmental Factor		Simple Correlation r	Explained Variance r^2
Country Size		.36*	.13
Social Heterogeneity		.08	.01
Sectionalism		.06	.00
Separation of Powers		.36*	.13
Effective Parliamentarism	$R^2 = .21$[b]	.01	.00
Weak Parliamentarism		.04	.00
Strong Presidentialism		−.32*	.10
Actual Polity Decentralization		.34*	.12
Federalism		.27*	.07

[a] $N = 91$ for all coefficients. Four parties (one each in Ecuador, Greece, Guatemala, and Peru) were not included in these analyses due to a lack of sufficient data for the measures of party decentralization.
[b] Using multiple regression, the "horizontal structure" dummy variables were combined with $R = .46$.
* Significant at the .05 level.

Table 5.1 presents the bivariate coefficients of relationship between party decentralization and each of the selected environmental variables. All relationships are in the expected direction, although several (and most notably social heterogeneity and sectionalism) are near zero.

The largest single relationships are those with country size, separation of powers, and actual polity decentralization. The positive relationship with separation of powers is joined by a significant negative relationship with strong presidential structure, as expected. When taken together, the four horizontal structures of government can "explain" 21

FIGURE 5.3 Party Decentralization by Horizontal Structure, With Countries Ranked by Mean Score

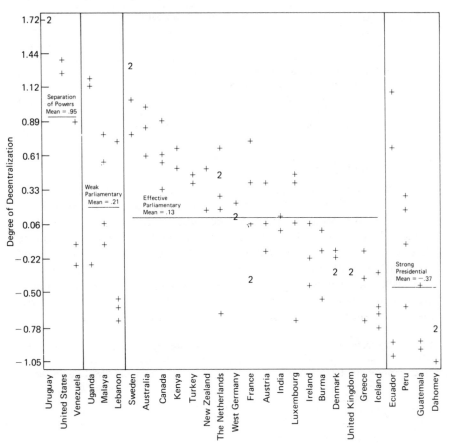

percent of the variance in party decentralization, as is displayed in Figure 5.3. (Note that two of the Venezuelan parties are far less decentralized than the American or Uruguayan parties, in spite of the separation of powers system.)

As predicted, the relationship with actual polity decentralization is larger than that with formal federalism. In fact, much of the relationship which does exist with federalism may be spurious, i.e., due to the fact that many federal systems are also effectively decentralized. This is revealed in the simple comparison of means presented in Table 5.2; the parties of the effectively decentralized systems are, on the average, significantly more decentralized than the parties of either formally federal (but not decentralized) or unitary systems, with the means for the latter two groups roughly equal to one another.

TABLE 5.2   Difference-of-Means Analysis for Party Decentralization in Actually Decentralized[a], Formally Federal (but Centralized), and Unitary Systems

Actually Decentralized		Formally Federal Only		Unitary
.60	>>	.10	=	.00
(n = 17)		(n = 13)		(n = 61)

>> The student's *t* statistic is significant at the .01 level.

= The student's *t* statistic is not significant at even the .10 level.

[a] All of the "actually decentralized" polities in our sample happen to be formally federal as well. The polities whose parties are included in the "Formally Federal Only" column are formally federal but *not* actually decentralized.

Explanatory Factors Combined

When combined by multiple regression, the size of the country and the vertical and horizontal structures of government can together explain 35 percent of the variance in party decentralization, as is revealed in Table 5.3. This amounts to more than half of the 68 percent variance that is environmentally explained. Consistent with their small bivariate relationships with party decentralization, though, social heterogeneity and sectionalism add negligibly to the overall explanation (and hence are not included in the table), suggesting that the influence often attributed to them in shaping party structure is apparently misplaced.

TABLE 5.3   Multiple Regression for Party Decentralization with Environmental Variables[a]

Environmental factor	Standardized Regression Coefficient
Country Size	.34*
Strong Presidentialism	−.47*
Separation of Powers	.19
Actual Polity Decentralization[c]	.24
b Federalism	−.27[wd]
Effective Parliamentarism	−.20
R^2 = .35 Adjusted R^2 = .30 N = 91	

* Significant at the .05 level.

[wd] Regression coefficient is in the opposite direction from that expected. See note 7.

[a] The results are for the equation whose adjusted R^2 is largest among those possible with combinations of the six independent variables. (See Chapter 2 for a discussion of this decision rule.) The R^2 is significant at the .05 level.

[b] It is always the case that only n−1 of n categories of a nominal variable are required to tap its complete explanatory power; the three horizontal structures included here contribute the total explanatory power of the four structural categories displayed in Figure 5.2.

[c] It is probable that some of the influence of polity decentralization has been attributed to other environmental factors in the model. The country size, for instance, is correlated at r^2 = .31 with polity decentralization; and for country size, strong presidentialism, and separation of powers combined, the R^2 = .38.

As predicted, presidentialism *with* an effective legislature (i.e., separation of powers) contributes positively to decentralization, while presidentialism *without* an effective legislature joins parliamentarism in promoting greater centralization.

Although *formal* federalism also appears to promote party centralization, it must be remembered that the coefficient reveals the contribution of federalism with actual decentralization (and the other environmental variables) controlled. We have already shown, by a comparison of means, that the parties in centralized federal systems are substantially more nationalized than the parties of effectively decentralized (*and federal*) systems and are generally as centralized as those of unitary systems. The lesson appears to be that a formal federal structure need not force decentralization upon the parties, *if* the federal structure is an empty "shell" without an *actual* distribution of power.[7] Even *with* effective decentralization of the polity, one or more of a system's parties may themselves avoid decentralized structures, as is suggested by the moderately sized regression coefficient and evidenced in the Venezuelan Christian Social party and the Kabaka Yekka party of Uganda (both of which have scores on the "centralized" side of the mean).

Because we have explained roughly one half of the 68 percent country-level variance in party decentralization, another half remains for speculation. Additional sources of explanation may be sought in other variables not considered here; for instance, students of Latin American parties (e.g., Payne, 1968) have suggested that the "status orientation" of national leaders may affect their parties' structures. But while additional environmental variables could undoubtedly contribute *some* further explanation, another possibility is that we have not yet adequately assessed the explanatory power of the variables already considered.

Everyone has heard of at least one situation where "the whole is bigger than the sum of its parts," and that may indeed be the case here. The multiple regression approach assumes that the individual (and "independent") contributions of the environmental variables can simply be added to arrive at the overall explanation. That approach may, and probably does, underestimate the effects of various combinations of environmental features. For example, the large size of system A may affect its parties' structures, and system B's parties may be affected by its separation of power, but the fact that system C has *both* of those features might affect its parties more (or perhaps less) profoundly than could be established simply by *adding* the effects of A's size and B's separation of powers. To put the argument another way: each particular *combination* of environmental features may itself make a separate contribution to the party's structure, above and beyond the simple sum of the features' individual effects.

To some, it may seem that we are leaning toward agreement with the idiographists, who would argue that every environment is unique and hence that generalization is folly. (See Chapter 2.) However, if we are suggesting that particular *configurations* of environmental features may themselves be important in explaining party structure, we are *not* suggesting the impossibility of generalizing across configurations or among the countries with similar configurations; only our relatively small sample of countries restricts our ability to do so here. And only the crudity of the available measures for several of the environmental variables keeps us from attempting a multiplicative model to capture interactive effects.

While we await the circumstances that will allow us to explain more fully the environmental influence on party structure, we must be cautious about rejecting plausible contributing factors; even social heterogeneity and sectionalism, neither of which gained support here *alone*, could be influential in a particular environmental configuration. For now,

FIGURE 5.4 Difference Between Party Decentralization Score and Predicted Score, With Countries Ranked by Mean Difference

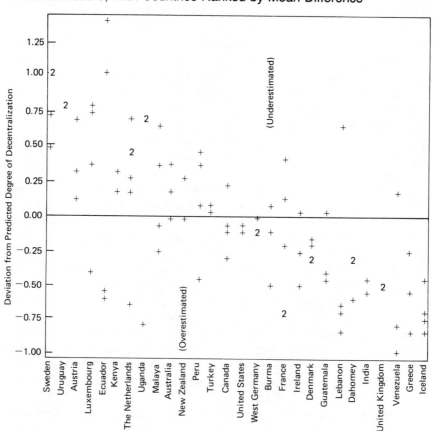

we must be content with our ability to explain half of the environmentally explained variance in party decentralization with just the size of the country and the vertical and horizontal structures of government.

The model employing those variables is quite successful in predicting the scores of some of the parties in the sample and unsuccessful in predicting others, as is indicated in Figure 5.4. The model *underestimates* the decentralization of the Swedish and Uruguayan parties, for instance, and *overestimates* decentralization for the parties of Iceland and, to some extent, India and Britain. But the model is on target in predicting the scores for the West German and American parties. In general, the model predicts for the "Western" parties better than for those of the "Third World," suggesting that future searches for additional explanatory variables might best be focused on the circumstances of the latter parties.

ANALYZING THE AMERICAN PARTIES

To the extent that our model is accurate, its ability to predict the American parties' high degree of decentralization should be less than heartening to those who argue for greater nationalization within the present context. It would appear that Ranney's claim of the American parties' being "entirely appropriate" for their setting is an accurate one. Large size, effective decentralization, and separation of powers have made this system particularly (some may say "uniquely") well suited to parties that are largely devoid of central control. Social heterogeneity and sectionalism merely complete the picture of an environment conducive to decentralization within the parties. Whatever the "most decentralizing" environmental configuration might be, the American brand must at least rank nearby.

What, then, can we say to those who would have the parties centralize? First, they may find some hope in the fact that 32 percent of the variance in party decentralization is *not* determined by country-level factors, though that hope is dampened by the fact that 68 percent *is*. Particularly troublesome is the fact that our sample offers no examples of similar environments where the parties are appreciably more nationalized. More encouraging, though, may be what is becoming a well-documented fact of *change* in the American environment. To the extent that those changes are in the direction conducive to greater nationalization, more centralized parties might be forthcoming, or at least *allowed*. A full discussion of those changes and their likely consequences for the parties awaits Chapter 7. First, though, we turn to another focus of responsible party proponents—legislative cohesion—in order to complete the comparative assessment of environmental impacts.

NOTES

1. This conceptualization of decentralization does *not* include the "horizontal" dimension of control over national-level organs by one or more national-level leaders. Though the ICPP data do include a variable called "leadership concentration," which taps the horizontal dimension, that variable is not included here because it is not directly relevant to the relationship between the national organs and those at lower levels of organization.

2. Though Payne's thesis was formulated with regard to Columbia, it applies to the Uruguayan situation as well.

3. The raw data for the area of the country are from the *World Handbook II* data set, originally from the 1965 *United Nations Demographic Handbook*.

4. The fractionalization measure is based on data from *Atlas Naradov Mira* and are available in the *World Handbook II* data set. Sectionalism is indicated by a three-point scale from Banks and Textor (1963), with "1" for negligible sectionalism, "2" for moderate sectionalism, and "3" for extreme sectionalism. (Note that the scores are reversed from the original data set.)

5. The basic data for the two dimensions of the horizontal structure variable are from Banks (1971) and Blondel (1973). Since the earmarks of the "classic parliamentary system" are legislative selection of the polity's effective head, dependency of the executive upon his party's holding the majority for his office, and the power of dissolution by the majority party leader, these are the indicators which we require before labeling one of the polities "parliamentary." Similarly, direct election of the effective executive by popular suffrage, lack of dependence upon party majority status for his security in office, and fixed legislative terms are the identifying characteristics of a "presidential" system. See Harmel (1981), P. 93. The data for executive selection and dependence on majority status are from Banks (1971), and those for power of dissolution are from Blondel (1973). The data for legislative effectiveness are from Banks (1971).

6. For the "formal federalism" variable, two data sets (Banks and Textor, 1963, and Blondel, 1969) and two authoritative books on the subject of federalism (Duchacek, 1970, and Riker, 1964) were consulted for lists of formally federal polities. For this study, formally federal polities were coded "2" and formally unitary polities were coded "1." Our measure of effective decentralization of power is adopted from Gurr's coding of polities in his data set as either "effectively decentralized" or "centralized." Using Gurr's data and personal knowledge about Rhodesia/Nyasaland, seven polities were coded with "2" for "decentralized," the other six being the United States, Australia, Canada, India, West Germany, and Uganda. (All were also coded as formally federal, along with Austria, Venezuela, Burma, and Malaya). The remaining polities were coded as "1" for "centralized."

7. Though the negative relationship between federalism and party decentralization is countertheoretical, it is likely a spurious relationship, i.e., federalism is strongly related to another environmental characteristic that actually causes the party decentralization.

APPENDIX TO CHAPTER 5

The following are the codes assigned to the American parties for the decentralization variables discussed on pages 59–60 of Chapter 5. The codes and descriptions relate to the parties during the period 1957–62. (Codes are described on page 60.)

Control over Communications   Democrats: 7   Republicans: 7

Neither party had what would be considered important means of communication within the party.

Administration of Discipline   Democrats: 4   Republicans: 4

There is virtually no exercise of discipline within either party.

Selection of Legislative Candidates   Democrats: 9   Republicans: 9

Neither national party had any say in the naming of candidates to run for congressional seats; this was normally done at the district level in primary elections.

Allocation of Funds   Democrats: 4   Republicans: 3

National party organs in both parties had a role in collecting and disbursing funds, including setting quotas for thé states. Though neither party enjoyed complete success in collecting the quotas, the Republicans did somewhat better than the Democrats.

Selection of National Party Leader   Democrats: 4   Republicans: 4

Both parties selected Presidential nominees at the national conventions, attended by delegates from the states.

Formulation of Party Policy   Democrats: 1   Republicans: 2

Both parties adopted platforms at the conventions; in addition, the Democrats used a Democratic Advisory Council during this period.

Nationalization of Structure   Democrats: 3   Republicans: 3

The national committees of the two parties consisted of representatives from state party organizations and had little authority over the state organs. During this period the state parties acted largely as autonomous organizations.

* More detailed descriptions are provided in Janda (1980a); note that the coding values have been reversed from the original scheme, so that the higher the value here, the higher the *de*centralization. While the values provided here are based on the coding scheme discussed on pages 59–60, the scores represented in Figures 5.1, 5.3, and 5.4 are composite standardized scores as discussed on page 44 and in note 4 on page 54.

6

The Environment and Party Cohesion

One purpose usually claimed for political parties is to shape public policy through concerted actions of their members in government positions. This purpose formed the basis of Edmund Burke's venerable definition of a party as "a body of men united, for promoting by their joint endeavours the national interest, upon some particular principle in which they are all agreed" (1975: 113). Although contemporary scholars recognize that parties vary in the degree of agreement on principles, they still recognize internal unity as one of the valued traits in a political party. Blondel (1978: 138) even cites "unity" as one of the four requirements of an *ideal* party. Unity is also preached in practical politics; witness the Preamble to the 1974 Charter of the Democratic Party: "We, the Democrats of the United States of America, united in common purposes, hereby rededicate ourselves to the principles which have historically sustained our Party." Moreover, Article One states that the party shall "Adopt and promote statements of policy" and "Work with Democratic public officials at all levels to achieve the objectives of the Democratic Party." (See the Democratic Party Charter reprinted in Appendix B.)

The most important test of party unity in democratic politics comes when party members vote on legislative issues. Party "cohesion" (or "unity") in the legislature is regarded as important because party voting is necessary for parties to shape public policy. Ozbudun reasons, "The more cohesive a party is, the greater is its role as a policy-making agent" (1970: 303).

Although it states other objectives as means to the end, the APSA Committee on Political Parties was ultimately most concerned about the level of cohesion within the American parties. The announced thesis of the Committee Report was that "Historical and other factors have caused the American two-party system to operate as two loose associations of state and local organizations, with very little national machinery and very little national cohesion." (1950: v). The Report saw the need for an *effective* party system, one which requires "first, that the parties are able to bring forth programs to which they commit themselves and, second, that the parties possess sufficient internal cohesion to carry out these programs." (Appendix A, p. 143). This call for commitment to party programs and legislative cohesion in supporting the party program became the hallmark of the "responsible party" school of reformers.

Almost immediately, the APSA Report came under attack for recommending that American parties become more programmatic and cohesive, in large part because the political environment in the United State simply would not support such parties.[1] Moreover, a different school of reformers felt that low cohesion was not as serious as the "unrepresentative" nature of American parties, and this alternative value came to dominate party reforms in the late 1950s and 1970s (Ranney, 1975: 44–46).

More recently, however, scholars have resurrected the ideals of the responsible party school. The "National Position Paper" issued by a group of scholars organized into the Committee on Party Renewal reflects these ideals. Reproduced in Appendix D, the ten-point program for party renewal aims at strengthening the parties to improve government accountability. Gerald Pomper, cochairman of this committee, has contended that environmental conditions have become more favourable to the emergence of such "responsible" parties (see Pomper, 1971). The concern of this chapter is to determine whether there is validity to the argument that party cohesion is primarily a function of the environment and thus lies beyond efforts at party reform.

MEASURING PARTY COHESION

The concept of cohesion centers on the extent of agreement among party members in voting on legislative issues. The *Congressional Quarterly* computes "party unity scores" as one way of measuring party cohesion. A party unity score expresses the percentage of time that a member votes in agreement with a majority of his party *on votes that split the parties*, when a majority of voting Democrats opposes a majority of voting Republicans. Aggregated over all party members in the House and the Senate, the mean party unity score is seen as an overall measure of cohesion within each party when party majorities take opposing stands. Figures 6.1 and 6.2 graph the mean party unit scores for Democrats and Republicans in the House and the Senate from 1954 through 1980.

The sawtooth appearance of the graphs in Figures 6.1 and 6.2 conveys an impression of haphazard volatility in party unity. The pattern is

FIGURE 6.1   Party Unity in the U.S. House, 1954–1980

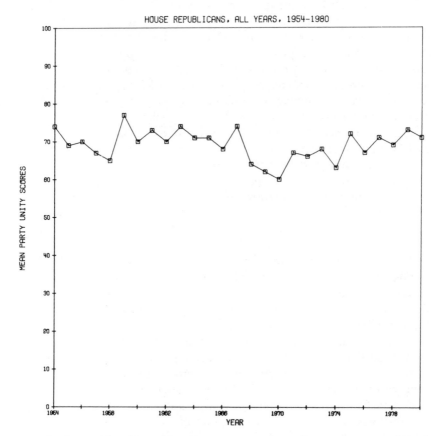

smoothed considerably when the mean party unity scores are plotted separately for election and nonelection years, as in Figures 6.3 and 6.4. These graphs quickly demonstrate that party unity tends to be somewhat higher in *non*election years than in election years. The average differences are not great (about 4 percentage points overall), but nonelection years almost always elicit higher party unity than election years. This may reflect the members' desire to vote constituency interests over party policy when running for reelection.[2] Whatever the reason for differences in party cohesion between odd and even years, the explanation must lie in the *structure* of the system and not in the idiosyncratic behavior of the separate parties in the two houses.

In fact, the patterns of party unity in the U.S. Congress have been similar for both parties in both chambers and rather stable since 1954. There is a trace of decline in party unity since 1954, especially for Republicans in the Senate, but the trend is not pronounced and even has shifted upward in recent years. For both parties, unity tends to be slightly greater in the House than in the Senate and slightly greater among

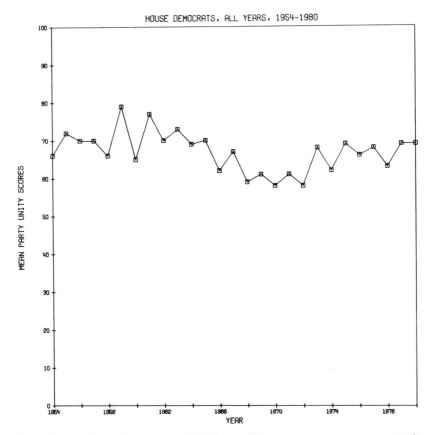

HOUSE DEMOCRATS, ALL YEARS, 1954-1980

Republicans than Democrats. But these differences are not great. At the extremes, the average Senate Democrat voted with a majority of his party and against a majority of Republicans 64 percent of the time compared to 69 percent party unity for the average House Republican.

How should we interpret these data on party cohesion? Some might regard figures upward of 60 percent party unity as evidence *for* cohesion rather than against it. One should remember, however, that a member who votes merely by chance will be on his party's side 50 percent of the time. Clearly, we need some standards for evaluating the extent of party cohesion in the U.S. Congress.

Unfortunately, there has not been much rigorous, systematic research on party cohesion across countries. Olson concludes:

> The many variations in voting procedures, conditions, and rules make it very difficult to obtain comparable evidence from a variety of parliaments; we are limited in the trends we can identify and in the degree of confidence we can place in our own observations (1980: 256–257).

FIGURE 6.2   Party Unity in the U.S. Senate, 1954–1980

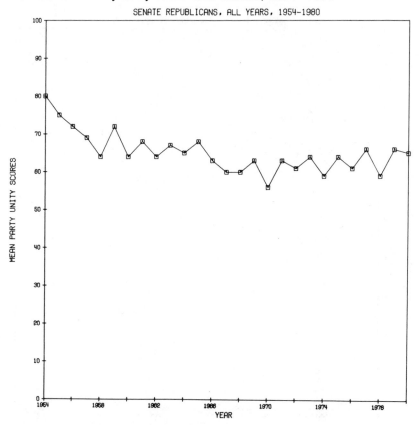

Olson limits his own analysis to data collected for 10 parties in France, Britain, West Germany, and the United States. He finds that only the French Radicals rank as low in party cohesion as the Democrats and the Republicans.

This chapter reports data from a more comprehensive study of party cohesion. The measure used differs somewhat from *Congressional Quarterly*'s party unity score by an adjustment for chance distributions of party support. This "index of cohesion" simply equals the absolute difference between the percentage of party members voting "yes" and the percentage voting "no" on a given vote. The measure ranges from 0.0 in the case of a party splitting 50/50 in supporting and opposing a bill to 1.0 in the case of all its members voting on the same side.[3] The level of party cohesion is simply the mean index of cohesion for all votes in the analysis.

For our study, the major difficulty in measuring party cohesion re-sults from the fact that the literature on political parties rarely reports

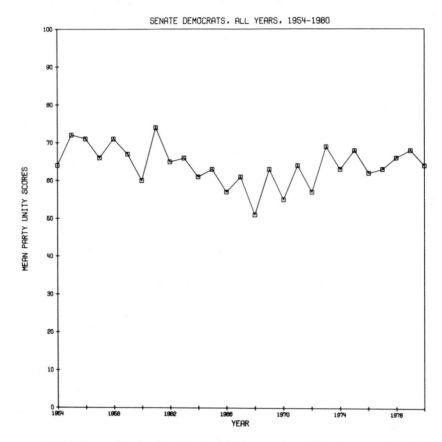

SENATE DEMOCRATS, ALL YEARS, 1954-1980

precise indices of cohesion for legislative voting. Where party divisions on legislative votes themselves were divulged, the index was calculated for the available votes. In the complete absence of empirical data, party cohesiveness was estimated according to this scheme:

Descriptive Statement	Divisions	Estimated Index
Completely cohesive	100/0	1.00
Highly cohesive	90/10	.80
Somewhat cohesive	80/20	.60
Not cohesive	70/30	.40
Divisive	60/40	.20
Highly divisive	50/50	.00

Even after resorting to estimating party cohesion from statements in the literature, we found that some parties still could not be coded because of inadequate information. In fact, it was possible to score only 67 of the 95 parties for this analysis.[4] The average level of cohesion among

FIGURE 6.3   Effect of Election Years on Party Unity in the U.S. House, 1954–1979

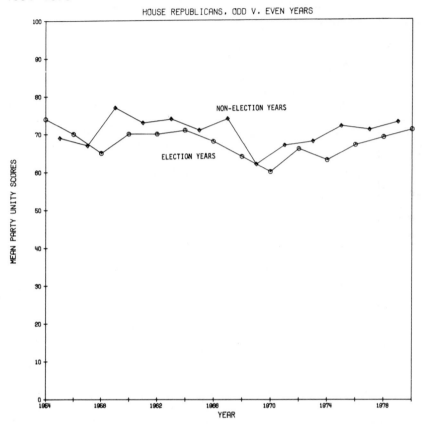

these parties was .84—far higher than the .63 and .65 scores reported respectively for the Democrats and the Republicans during the 1957–62 period by Turner and Schneier.[5]

These estimates of party cohesion for the Democrats and the Republicans differ from the party unity scores in that they include *all* recorded votes, not just those in which a majority of one party opposes a majority of the other. Thus the index of cohesion, despite correcting for chance distributions of party support, yields values coincidentally similar to party unity scores because of the inclusion of unanimous and nearly unanimous roll call votes. The index of cohesion was chosen over the party unity measure because the index of cohesion allows for assessing cohesion in multiparty legislatures, in which party unity votes cannot be defined as just one party opposed to another.

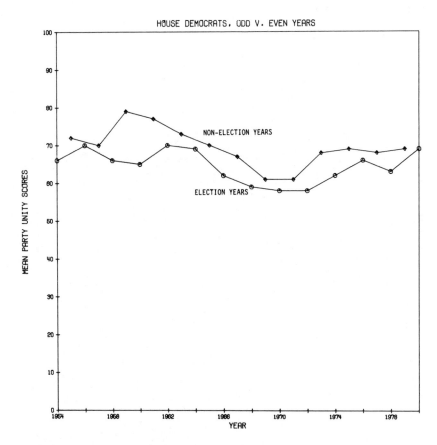

HOUSE DEMOCRATS, ODD V. EVEN YEARS

ASSESSING ENVIRONMENTAL EFFECTS ON PARTY COHESION

Mild environmental effects on party cohesion can be seen in the influence of election years on party unity among Democrats and Republicans. Even more powerful effects can be attributed to the country environment. In particular, America's environment is commonly cited as determining the low level of cohesion within the two parties. Blank's evaluation is typical:

> Given the framework of the decentralized governmental system operating in the United States, the lack of highly disciplined and centralized parties is not surprising. The parties simply reflect the government as a whole (1980: 235).

To what degree do parties in the same country display similar levels of

FIGURE 6.4 Effect of Election Years on Party Unity in the U.S. Senate, 1954–1979

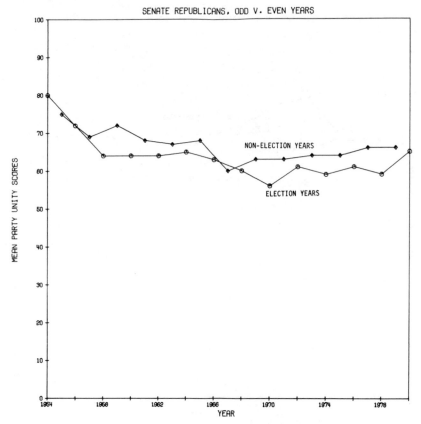

SENATE REPUBLICANS, ODD V. EVEN YEARS

cohesion, thereby reflecting environmental influences, and how do American parties actually compare to the cohesion of parties in other countries? The effect of country on party cohesion is portrayed in Figure 6.5, which plots the cohesion scores for 67 parties in 21 countries ranked by their mean party cohesion scores.

Our measure of cohesion was modified for presentation in Figure 6.5. Because the parties bunched together at the high cohesion end of the scale, we separated them somewhat by squaring the scores. Thus, if one party had a score of .95 and another a score of .90 (a difference of .05), the difference became .09 (.90 versus .81) after squaring. This technique of transforming variables is useful when small differences at one end of a scale have greater significance than comparable differences at the other end.[6] We see that the parties do tend to cluster somewhat by country, with 58 percent of the variance in cohesion scores explained by country environment, whatever "environment" might entail. The countries showing the lowest party cohesion are Uruguay, Guatemala,

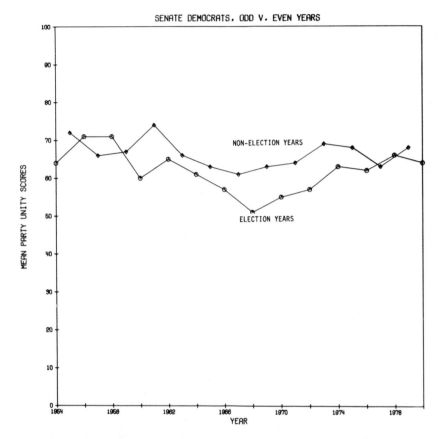

Burma, and the United States. Those which show the highest cohesion are the United Kingdom, Malaya, Denmark, and West Germany. Some countries (Austria, Burma, and the Netherlands) harbor parties that differ greatly in legislative cohesion, while others (including the United States) have parties that show little if any difference. Moreover, a bloc of 12 countries at the upper right of Figure 6.5 features parties with little variance and very high cohesion. What, if anything, do these countries have in common to produce such high party cohesion?

EXPLAINING ENVIRONMENTAL EFFECTS ON PARTY COHESION

How much of the country-specific variance in party cohesion can be recovered with theoretical explanations of environmental effects on legislative voting? As usual, we will consider various factors that have been

FIGURE 6.5 Degree of Party Cohesion, by Country

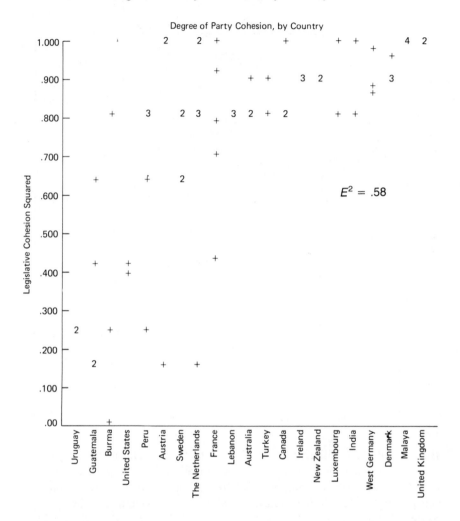

Degree of Party Cohesion, by Country

$E^2 = .58$

hypothesized as system-level causes of party cohesion before constructing a multicausal explanation.

Individual Explanatory Factors

Many scholars have ventured explanations of party cohesion across nations, but few have specialized in its study. In their analysis of congressional voting, Turner and Schneier (1970) devoted some attention to the sources of party cohesion across nations, and Ozbudun (1970) undertook a general investigation of party cohesion from a comparative perspective. We rely heavily on their work in our discussion of six factors that have been proposed as causes of party cohesion: presidential government, federalism, multiple parties, ideological polarization, single-member districts, and legislative effectiveness.

Most authors agree that the structure of the *relationship between the executive and the legislature* has an important effect on party cohesion. Where the executive and the legislators are separately elected, as in a presidential form of government, the government leadership does not depend on party unity in the legislature. In parliamentary systems, on the other hand, the executive is selected by the parliament and depends on continued support from the parliamentary majority. This puts a premium on party unity. Ozbudun believes that "parliamentary government is a sufficiently strong factor to produce cohesive legislative parties, provided that it operates in a two-party or moderate two-party system" (1970: 363). The general proposition is that party cohesion is lower in presidential systems than in parliamentary systems.

Another factor that has been blamed for the low cohesion of American parties is the *federal structure* of government. (Rossiter, 1963, and Key, 1964). Just as federalism promotes devolution of party power to state organs, it also provides legislators with sources of support and foci for allegiance that may compete with the national party. Hence, many students would agree with Blank: "A modification in the [U.S.] federal system would be necessary to produce increased levels of party cohesion and centralization of authority" (1980: 235). Generalizing from the American situation, we may expect to find lower party cohesion in the federal systems in our sample than in the unitary systems.

Turner and Schneier (1970) have proposed that the *number of parties* in a system is related to their levels of cohesion, and this relationship is suggested by Loewenberg and Patterson (1979: 224) as well. The underlying argument is that multiparty (as opposed to two-party) politics produces smaller and more homogeneous parties, with greater intraparty cohesion the natural consequence.

As a "sociopolitical" explanation, Ozbudun (1970) proposes that class *polarization* within society correlates with party cohesion. There is some ambiguity, however, about what Ozbudun means by "class polarization." In places he speaks about the way "the party system reflects class divisions in the society," but in other places he refers to the social homogeneity of the individual party; the latter usage makes polarization a party-level rather than a system-level factor (1970: 343–344). We will interpret "class polarization" as ideological polarization, measured by the range of party ideologies in the parliament as a weighted function of the size of the delegation.[7] Thus the greater the spread in party strength along the ideological continuum, the greater the ideological polarization, and (presumably) the greater the party cohesion.

American scholars often cite the election of United States congressmen from *single-member districts* as a major factor in their independence from party leadership (see, for example, Fenno, 1978: 31–32). Congressmen run for election individually, and they are able to forge their own links with constituents to increase their chances of winning. Data show that more than 90 percent of incumbent representatives win reelection along with more than 80 percent of incumbent senators.[8] Although the number of candidates elected is not often suggested as a general factor explaining party cohesion across nations, we will include it in our analysis, distinguishing between countries that elect their legislators from single-member districts and those that send multi-member delegations to the legislature.[9]

Finally, some legislative scholars have posited a correlation between party cohesion and the *effectiveness of the legislature*. Mezey (1979: 77, 102, and 138), for instance, distinguishes between legislatures with "strong" policy-making powers and those with "modest" or no policy-making powers. He notes that those with strong powers tend to show *less* party discipline. Mezey's observations conform to Polsby's (1975: 291–292) argument that legislatures that "transform" the executive's proposals to their own liking before enacting them into law are apt to feature fluid voting coalitions and decentralized parties. The causal connection between legislative effectiveness and party cohesion is not clear, however. Is it that effective legislatures make for low party cohesion, or that low cohesion makes for effective legislatures? Schwarz and Shaw (1976: 398) contend that the undisciplined nature of the American parties has enhanced the undeniable effectiveness of the Congress in modifying presidential proposals, representing public opinion, and initiating legislation. Although the long-run effect of low party cohesion may strengthen legislative effectiveness, it seems that the causal connection in the short run goes *from* the legislature's role in the political system *to* party cohesion. Thus we expect that the more effective the legislature, the *lower* the party cohesion.[10]

TABLE 6.1   Bivariate Correlations between Environmental Variables and Party Cohesion for 67 Parties in 21 Countries

Environmental Factor	Simple Correlation r	Explained Variance r^2
Presidential system	−.53*	.28
Federalism	.05	.00
Number of parties	.00	.00
Ideological polarization	−.04	.00
Single-member districts	−.11	.01
Legislative effectiveness	.26*	.07

* Significant at the .05 level.

The six environmental factors just described have all been advanced to explain differences in party cohesion in legislative voting across nations. As indicated in Table 6.1, not all the simple correlations between these factors and party cohesion are as large as expected nor are they even in the expected direction.

Despite causal claims in the literature, federalism, the number of parties, ideological polarization, and single-member districts bear no simple relationships to party cohesion. Of all the various factors suggested as causes of party cohesion across nations, only the presence of a presidential system and legislative effectiveness are significantly correlated with the index of cohesion. The effect of presidential government is exactly as expected, strongly depressing party cohesion. The correlation of −.53 is by far the highest in the table, which is consistent with the literature's judgment that the legislative-executive structure is the most important cause of party cohesion (see Epstein, 1975: 265–266). The effect of legislative effectiveness, on the other hand, is the direct opposite of what the literature predicts. The more effective the legislature, the *higher* the party cohesion. We will examine this anomaly more closely later.

Explanatory Factors Combined

As we have seen in earlier chapters, variables may have more explanatory power when joined together than when used separately. In this case, the only two variables that combine fruitfully are parliamentarism and legislative effectiveness. The regression equation built from these two factors is reported in Table 6.2.

TABLE 6.2   Multiple Regression for Party Cohesion with Environmental Variables

Environmental Factor	Standardized Regression Coefficient
Presidential system	−.66*
Legislative effectiveness	−.22
R^2 = .32	N = 67

* Significant at the .05 level.

The results of the regression analysis show that 32 percent of the variance in party cohesion can be explained by the legislative-executive structure and the effectiveness of the legislature in the political system. As found in the analysis of the individual factors, the presence of presidential government decreases party cohesion, even when controlling for legislative effectiveness. But the sign for legislative effectiveness is switched when presidential government is controlled. The impact of legislative effectiveness now *also* depresses party cohesion. This effect was not seen before because of the negative relationship ($r = -.52$) between presidential government and legislative effectiveness (meaning that effective legislatures are more likely to be found in *parliamentary* systems). Because parliamentarism is strongly predictive of high cohesion, the impact of legislative effectiveness is apparently reversed. But the regression analysis reveals that the prevailing theory is conditionally correct; party cohesion is lower in effective legislatures, but only when legislative structure is held constant.

FIGURE 6.6 Plot of Parties' Cohesion Scores by Countries Within Different Legislative Environments

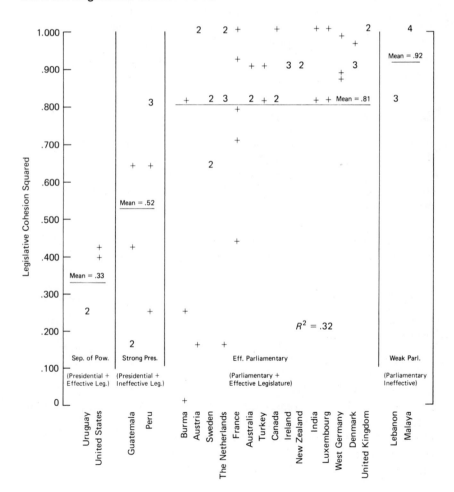

In the regression analysis of Chapter 5, we found it theoretically useful to combine the categories of "legislative structure" and "legislative effectiveness" in order to produce four "horizontal governmental structures." Here we have treated the two variables separately in order to maximize consistency with the existing theory concerning party cohesion. It is again useful to combine the variables in order to provide a graphic demonstration of the effects of legislative-executive structure and legislative effectiveness. In Figure 6.6, the countries are ranked by mean party cohesion within each of the four types of legislative environment. The plot of party cohesion scores shows a definite increase in mean party cohesion as one progresses across the types of legislative environments. The least cohesive parties are found in presidential systems with effective legislatures (i.e., "separation of power" systems, in the terminology of Chapter 5), exemplified by Uruguay and the United States. Presidential systems with ineffective legislatures ("strong presidential" systems) have parties that are somewhat more cohesive. The combination of parliamentary government and effective legislatures ("effective parliamentary" systems) is the most common environment for this sample of parties and produces parties that are substantially more cohesive. Finally, the most cohesive parties are found in the two countries, Lebanon and Malaya, with parliamentary systems and ineffective legislatures (the "weak parliamentary" systems).

This analysis of environmental effects on party cohesion suggests that two variables—legislative-executive structure and legislative effectiveness—can be used in multiple regression to explain 32 percent of the total variance in party cohesion. This is over half of the 58 percent due to country identity and indicates that the legislative environment in particular has much to say about the cohesiveness of the parties which operate within it.

ANALYZING THE AMERICAN PARTIES

Critics of the responsible party model of programmatic and cohesive parties have contended that the American political environment is not conducive to such parties. They argue that cohesive parties are the products of parliamentary systems, which demand party unity to keep governments in power. The American presidential system, on the other hand, allows the President to serve a four-year term regardless of defeats in congressional voting. Our analysis indicates that party cohesion *does* tend to be very low in presidential systems and especially in those with effective legislatures.

This evidence tends to support critics of the responsible party model who believe that the American political environment is not suited to cohesive parties. But other evidence suggests that higher levels of party cohesion are possible in presidential systems. In fact, higher cohesion was the case in the United States itself at an earlier time. The study of party cohesion in Congress from 1886 to 1966 by Brady, Cooper, and Hurly (1979: 384–385, 393) found that party voting was highest in the 1890–1910 period and lowest in the period 1940–1966. The mean cohesion for the Democrats for 1890 to 1910 was .74, compared to .65 for the period 1940–1966. The Republican cohesion dropped from .78 to .68 over the same period. Moreover, these drops in cohesion came in spite of more bipartisan voting, which tends to raise cohesion scores.

Despite this message from United States history, the more recent cross-national data offer little comfort for supporters of the responsible party model. They cannot point to contemporary countries with nonparliamentary systems and effective legislatures which produce high levels of cohesion. If reformers wish to make the American parties more cohesive, they will have to do it *in spite of* the country's legislative-executive structure.

Avenues may still be available to those who would pursue more cohesive parties despite the barriers posed by our presidential system. There are two ways in which to proceed toward that objective. One is to pursue reforms at the party level, wringing as much influence as possible out of party-level causes of legislative cohesion. Our analysis suggests that country-specific factors account for almost 60 percent of the variance in party cohesion, but that still leaves some 40 percent due to party-level factors. France offers a good example of party factors at work. As depicted in Figure 6.6, the five French parties display different levels of cohesion for the period under study. The Communist party is the most cohesive, with a score of 1.0. Ranking slightly lower is the Socialist party, followed by the Gaullists, then the Popular Republican Movement (MRP), and then the Radical Socialists. Interestingly, this ranking is almost identical to the parties' combined scores for organizational complexity and decentralization of power, the two aspects of party organization considered in preceding chapters.

We know from previous research that these two party-level variables are mutually independent causes of party cohesion. Janda's (1979b) study of the effects of party organization on party performance found that party complexity is positively related to cohesion while decentralization is negatively related. As shown in Chapter 4, the American parties were already about average among all parties in complexity during the 1957–62 period so there would seem to be little room for increasing party cohesion by increasing complexity. But as shown in Chapter 5, the American parties were also *extremely* decentralized.

If power within the parties were more concentrated at the national level and if the Democratic and the Republican leaders in Congress shared in the greater power (as proposed in the APSA Report, Appendix A, p. 148), one likely consequence would be a higher degree of party cohesion in congressional voting. Indeed, Brady, Cooper, and Hurley account for the higher cohesion in the period 1890–1910 in terms of the centralized leadership of the Speaker of the House and the importance of the party caucus. Moreover, they point out that the 1940–1966 period of low cohesion featured neither centralized leadership nor a strong party caucus (1979: 392).[11]

Thus, if the American parties were better organized and more centralized, the argument goes, they would display more unity in congressional voting. This approach to increasing party cohesion focuses on changing party-level factors rather than changing the environment. Of course, the environment also determines a considerable amount of the variance in complexity and power, but again not all of it. If party organization and centralization were increased within the limits of environmental constraints, then some increase in party cohesion should follow. This is the crux of the argument for increasing party cohesion through party reform. We will consider further the environmental constraints on such reform and the possible changes in these constraints in Chapter 7.

The other avenue for increasing party cohesion would lead to changing the environment. As demonstrated by the cross-national analyses in the preceding chapters, the environment within which parties operate accounts for considerable portions of the variance in some party characteristics. It explains 57 percent of organizational complexity, 68 percent of party decentralization, and 58 percent of legislative cohesion. Because of the demonstrated influence of the environment, it may not be enough for those who would make the American parties more responsible to work only at the party level. To the extent possible, efforts should be directed toward changing, or at least "tuning up," the very environment that is so potent in shaping the parties.

REFORMING PARTIES BY REFORMING THE ENVIRONMENT

While the United States' constitutional structure seems immune to the actions of party reformers, the political environment as a whole is not. The portion that is dependent on state and federal statutes can be more easily changed. The history of party primaries provides an example of such environmental change. Crotty's account of party primaries notes that the Kentucky and the Mississippi Legislatures provided for optional primaries as early as 1892. By 1900, two-thirds of the states had adopted some form of primary laws, and only four states lacked primaries for state or local races by 1917 (1977: 203–207). It took until 1955, however, for primaries to spread to the last state, Connecticut (Sorauf, 1980: 204). Despite the appearance of a complete conversion to the election of party candidates in primary elections, states often tinkered with the coverage of offices included under primary legislation. This was especially true for presidential primaries to select delegates for the parties' national conventions. Peaking at 27 in 1916, the number of states with presidential primaries declined rapidly and fluctuated between 15 and 18 from 1924 to 1968, after which the number soared to a new peak of 35 in 1980 (Rubin, 1980: 129). Thus primaries have come and gone according to the winds of party reform.

The great effect of the primary system on the structure of American parties and presidential politics has been noted by many writers.[12] Working to change the system in order to change its parties is an established technique of party reformers. Some authors seeking to "democratize" the internal workings of the parties have labored for more primaries as a means to that end. The set of recommendations for strengthening the parties proposed by the Committee for Party Renewal also recognizes the importance of changing the environment as a means of party change. Four of their ten recommendations (see Appendix D, p. 170) involve changing the environment through the enactment of statutes:

2. Providing public funding to parties rather than candidates
3. Giving parties more freedom in financing their operations
4. Altering state laws to provide for party caucuses and conventions (rather than primaries alone)
9. Amending federal law to provide regular access to television for the major parties

These recommendations carry enormous consequences for both major parties. Items 2 and 9 have potential for increasing the importance of the national party organization. Items 4 and to a lesser extent 3 are directed toward strengthening the party organizations at the state and local levels. The net effect of these statutory changes, if enacted, promises to increase significantly the parties' organizational complexity and especially to lessen their present condition of extreme decentralization.

The question arises whether these statutory changes in the narrow political environment would be consonant with the broader environment of American society and politics. In democracies, parties cannot make statutory changes alone, or in a vacuum. Such changes must "fit" the larger environment and must appeal to a broader audience than the parties themselves. The statutory changes that would lead to strengthening the American parties may be no more welcome in this environment than strong parties themselves. The growth in the use of primaries shows that the environment has been receptive to even weaker (rather than stronger) parties. Yet, other signs point to broader changes in the environment that the parties could presumably help to further and then use to their advantage. Those changes and their potential impact on the parties are the stuff of Chapter 7.

NOTES

1. See Julius Turner, "Responsible Parties: A Dissent from the Floor," *American Political Science Review*, Vol. 45 (March 1951), pp.143–152; Austin Ranney, "Toward a More Responsible Two Party System: A Commentary," *American Political Science Review*, vol. 45 (June 1951), pp. 488–499; Murray S. Stedman and Herbert Sonthoff, "Party Responsibility: A Critical Inquiry," *Western Political Quarterly*, vol. 4 (September 1951), pp. 454–468; and T. William Goodman, "How Much Political Party Centralization Do We Want?" *Journal of Politics*, vol. 13 (November 1951), pp. 536–561. Ranney's critique about the unsuitability of the American environment for responsible parties is particularly sharp.

2. It also may reflect the tendency of freshmen legislators to take cues from the party leadership immediately after their election the preceding year. The difference between party unity in election and nonelection years poses some tantalizing research questions for the future.

3. Some readers may recognize this as the index of cohesion originated by Stuart A. Rice. See Lee Anderson, Meredith Watts, and Allan Wilcox, *Legislative Roll Call Analysis* (Evanston, Ill.: Northwestern University Press, 1966).

4. We actually scored 70 of the 95 parties, but we limited the analysis to countries with more than one party to permit the expression of variance within countries.

5. Julius Turner and Edward V. Schneier (1970), p. 21. Turner and Schneier report average cohesion scores for selected sessions of the U.S. House of Representatives. These scores are for the 1959 session, which is the only one they studied between 1957 and 1962.

6. The effect of the transformation is to pull apart parties clustered at the high end while pushing them together at the low end. In the process, it alters the statistics of the distribution. The mean for the original cohesion scores was .84, and the standard deviation was .20. After squaring, the mean was .75, and the standard deviation was .27.

7. The formula for computing the amount of ideological polarization first computes the difference between a party's ideological position and the mean ideology score for all the parties in the system. This difference is then multiplied by the proportion of seats the party holds in the legislature. The products are summed over all parties in a system to yield the ideological polarization score. This formula is similar to that used by Sigelman and Yough, but they weight the ideological differences by the proportion of votes won rather than seats won. See Lee Sigelman and Syng Nam Yough (1978).

8. *Congressional Quarterly* (1978), p. 9. The proportion of incumbent senators who lost in reelection attempts has fluctuated over the years and dropped under 50 percent in 1980.

9. Using the Blondel scale of electoral systems described in Chapter 4, note 18, we scored the eleven countries coded "3" and "4" as having single-member districts.

10. We use the Banks and Textor measure of the status of the legislature to indicate legislative effectiveness. They define as "fully effective" a legislature that "performs normal legislative function as reasonably 'co-equal' branch of national government." A "partially effective" legislature showed tendency toward domination by executive, or otherwise partially limited in effective exercise of legislative function. They also have two other categories, "largely ineffective" and "wholly ineffective," but none of our countries fell into those categories. In our analysis, an "effective legislature" is one they rate as "fully effective." See Banks and Textor (1963), p. 110. Most of our data came from Banks and Textor, but missing data were coded from Arthur F. Banks (1971).

11. Although the caucus was revived in the Democratic party in the House in 1971 and exercised considerable power by deposing three committee chairmen in 1975, the authors argue that the "new" caucus has not functioned as an instrument of party leadership like the "old" caucus and thus has not contributed to the cohesion of the Democratic party in congressional voting. Moreover, the increase in the Speaker's powers in the 1970s has been countered by a weakening in the power of committee chairmen and a decentralization of power to subcommittees.

12. Sorauf notes six threats that primaries pose to the well-being of party organization (1980: 212–213). For a more positive evaluation of the contributions of primaries to party politics, see Hugh A. Bone, *American Politics and the Party System* 4th Ed. (New York: McGraw-Hill, 1971), pp. 279–282.

7

The American Parties in a Changing Environment

ENVIRONMENTAL LIMITS TO STRONG, PROGRAMMATIC PARTIES: INFERENCES FROM CROSS-NATIONAL ANALYSES

In Chapters 3 through 6, we investigated the relationship of environmental factors to four major features of "responsible" political parties: (1) ideological clarity, (2) organization (or "complexity"), (3) centralization of power, and (4) cohesion in legislative voting. In our cross-national analyses, all of these features were found to be influenced to a substantial degree by the party's environment. That fact, as well as several of the specific findings, have clear relevance to the American parties and especially to the central question of this book: whether the American parties *could* become stronger and more programmatic, even if they wanted to.

In Chapter 3, two-partyism and plurality elections were found to be closely related to a limited ideological choice in the party system (with the number of parties and the type of electoral system together able to explain nearly one-half of the variance in ideological distance). Although that would seem to bode ill for the ability of the American parties to offer greater ideological clarity in their present context, a comparison with the British system alone revealed that the American parties *already* provide as much "distance" as their English counterparts. We concluded that, with the parties' "moving apart" neither likely nor apparently necessary, the American parties might clarify the choices they already provide by enforcing greater legislative cohesion, with stronger national parties a precondition.

In Chapter 4, we found that 57 percent of the variance in party organization could be attributed to the environment within which parties operate. Of six characteristics found to be conducive to greater complexity, the American environment possessed four of them: a large population, broad suffrage, a modern economy, and close party competition.

The American parties were found to be somewhat below the level of organizational complexity "predicted" by their environmental characteristics, suggesting that there was still some room for the parties to develop their organizational structures, within the limits of environmental constraints. But the data also indicated that the Democrats and the Republicans in the early 1960s were not seriously deficient in their organizational structures compared to parties in other countries with similar environments. Increasing the parties' organizational complexity (at least as we have measured it) alone would appear to be a misplaced focus for reformers seeking stronger national parties.

In contrast, Chapters 5 and 6 revealed that the American parties ranked very low on both centralization and cohesion, making them prime targets for reformers' attention. The analyses of environmental constraints, however, suggested that meaningful change on those dimensions could be quite difficult, if not impossible. Separation of powers alone appears to place a severe limit on legislative cohesion; and it joins with polity decentralization and, especially, large country size in encouraging party decentralization. Nevertheless, we did find room for more cohesion than the American parties now possess, even within the separation of powers framework, *if* the parties can find the means for strengthening their national organs. Short of moving to a different environment, however, the latter itself might seem an impossible mission.

It is our purpose in this chapter to establish the extent to which the parties already are in a "different environment" than was the case even a few decades ago, and then to consider the effect of that new environment on the parties and their prospects for the future.

THE CALL AND THE EARLY RESPONSE

When the APSA Committee on Political Parties made its report on the state of the American party system in 1950, it called for a number of reforms intended to "democratize" the internal workings of those parties while strengthening their national organizations as well. Whether in direct response to the Report or, as is more likely, to other demands, both parties did "open up" their nominating processes through greater use of the direct primary; the Democrats gave convention delegates a larger role in the selection of national committee members; and both parties have recently encouraged the use of "affirmative action" in the selection of delegates and officers. Until very recently, however, the other major goal, *strengthening* the national parties, went largely unattended.

That in itself need not surprise us, given what we have already said about the American environment—hardly suited to more centralized parties. If countries do get the· kind of parties they need and want, then weak, decentralized parties might have been expected to prosper in a large and decentralized United States. And prospering is what they seemed to be doing—until recently, that is.

By 1970, signs had begun to appear that the parties might be in serious trouble with the electorate. Americans have never been known for their great love of parties (see Gelb and Palley, 1975, and Ranney, 1975), but until the 1960s they had at least seen them as necessary, had used them, and had identified with them. In his 1970 book, Burnham noted a recent, marked increase in split-ticket voting, more massive than would even accompany a normal period of realignment. By 1975, Ladd and Hadley were noting that "the proportion of voters describing themselves as independents, rather than as Republicans or Democrats, has increased notably since the 1950's" and, even more alarming for the future of the parties, "among the young and the college educated today, independents are the largest 'party,' their numbers exceeding those of self-identified Democrats and Republicans" (1975: 15). By the late 1970s it had become commonplace to see references, both in the popular and the professional media, to the "decline," "decay," or even impending "demise" of the American parties.

But why? What had *changed* to cause this depressing state of party affairs? The first response must be: not the parties! While both parties had experienced some reform by the time the decline was first becoming apparent, they maintained hardly less "decentralization" or "openness" than had been the case in the '30s, '40s, and '50s. It seems to us that the answer lies instead with change in the parties' *environment*. The parties remained substantially the same, but the environment was changing profoundly. Further, it seems to us that the environment was changing on some of the dimensions most critical for shaping party structure. If we are right, then the American environment of the '60s and '70s may have been more receptive to stronger national parties than had ever been the case before, including the very period when the APSA Committee was writing its call. In a sense, the American parties had been "moved" to a different environment.

THE CHANGED ENVIRONMENT: DIMENSIONS AFFECTING PARTY DECENTRALIZATION

What Has Not Changed

Before detailing what we see as important changes in the American environment, we must note some important features that *have not* changed, or at least not in the direction that would promote party centralization. One such feature is the system of separation of powers, which we found to be associated with both decentralization and lack of legislative cohesion. There can be little doubt that the separation of the legislative party from the executive has severely limited attempts to enforce discipline, both upon the legislator and the more localized party organs to which he is more directly responsible. And rather than being weakened, the effectiveness of the separation may actually have been widened by recent events. As Everson argues:

> If the Congress is to be seen as an effective and independent branch of government, the odds are that it must do so *in opposition* to the president.... In the wake of recent events which called into question uncritical acceptance of presidential government, it is unlikely that Congress will accept a passive role (1980: 277).

If a system of more unified power and shared fate is necessary for truly *centralized* parties, then short of the constitutional revision that is so unlikely, centralized parties will remain just as unlikely here. Nonetheless, it may be possible for the American parties to be *less decentralized* (and perhaps much less so) than has been the case in the past, even within the separation of powers system.

Another challenge to the formation of strong parties comes from a long history of "antiparty feelings"[1] in this country. In his Farewell Address, George Washington warned his countrymen of the "baneful, divisive effects of faction"; his words seem to have echoed through the past two centuries of Americans "putting up with" parties as a necessary evil. Dennis's (1966 and 1975) studies of Wisconsin voters have shown a repeatedly negative attitude toward parties, and a survey asking a national sample to rank a list of institutions according to their "likes" found the parties at the bottom of the list.[2]

If *parties* are merely "put up with," what prospects might there be for finding support for *stronger* parties? Almost four decades ago, Schattschneider (1942: 209–10) found it "not unreasonable" to think that the public could be educated on the good points of stronger parties. While the public has not yet been convinced (as evidenced in the Dennis surveys), it would be difficult to argue that anyone has seriously tried to persuade them. If we are right in the analysis which follows, then events may have already begun to teach the obsolesence of *weak* parties. Whether this can be converted into positive feelings for *stronger* parties may depend in part on our experiences with the other institutions that are vying for rights to perform what have traditionally been the parties' roles. (More on them later.)

What Has Changed

Technological society. We have already found evidence for the claims that America's large size and polity decentralization may have contributed to the development of such decentralized parties. Though not finding supporting evidence here, we have also noted that students of American parties have often pointed to the decentralizing influence of the country's heterogeneous population and especially its sectionalized politics. It has been claimed that taken together, these environmental features have provided a configuration "second to none" (or at least second only to Uruguay's) in promoting party decentralization. But even if that *was* the case in the past, advances in transportation and communication technologies may have significantly lessened the effects of size and heterogeneity, while paving the way for more nationalized politics and more centralized government.

While America's large and heterogeneous population may have preserved, or even guaranteed, the effective decentralization of both polity and parties *in the past*, space age technology has made distances "shorter" and differences "smaller." Buckholts has nicely summarized the effects of moving to the advanced stages of industrialization:

> The rapid development of the airplane, along with telecommunications, in this century has been the chief reason that we tend to view the globe as diminished in size and that events and people are much closer and of greater concern to us (1966: 314).

And what is true globally is exaggerated in the American context, where "Southern" problems are now Northern problems, too, and where Los Angeles's smog and New York's crime are shared with television viewers in Iowa.

And not only has advanced industrialization made short-term travel and communications easier; it has actually encouraged more long-term contact with more than one area of the country. The industrial age has brought with it a particularly mobile class of professionals, technicians, and administrators (see Smith and Zopf, 1976: 546), who tend to move from place to place for job-related reasons. And the tremendous increase in the proportion of high school graduates who have attended college, often in other states, has provided many young adults with long-term "outside" experiences that were unusual in earlier generations. In all, it has been estimated that roughly one-sixth of the population now changes state residence in the span of a decade (Heller, 1966), which could not help affecting the balance between the parochial interests which have so colored our politics in the past and the more cosmopolitan, "national" interests and affections which could help to shape our future. Cumulatively, these changes have brought about a reduction in the potency of the "centrifugal forces" which may have contributed to the *need* for decentralized political institutions, including parties, in the earlier periods of our history.

Nationalization of politics. Whether true cross-nationally or *not* (as suggested by our own analyses), sectionalism has often been cited as a prime contributor to the decentralization of America's parties (e.g., see Keefe, 1972; Schattschneider, 1942; and Sorauf, 1980). Sectionalism, it is argued, requires that the more localized organs of the party, as well as the representatives of the party in Congress, be allowed to respond to sectional demands even when they conflict with national party positions. And when sectional one-party dominance is a fact of politics, as it has been in the Southern and Northeastern sections of this country, national organization is rendered extremely difficult, if not impossible. "A national alignment creates a demand for political organization through-out the country," Schattschneider has argued (1965: 435); "whereas sec-tionalism depresses national organizations."

But over recent decades, politics has become more "nationalized" and less regionalized behaviorally, as evidenced in both electoral and congressional behavior. As Ladd summarizes the voting trends:

> In contrast to the extreme sectionalism of the four decades after 1890, the four since 1930 have seen a nationalization of politics, or, as E. E. Schatt-schneider puts it, the substitution of 'a national political alignment every-where. . . .' Schattschneider added a qualification to *everywhere*: 'except in the South.' We can now drop this qualification, for while the South remains a deviating region in which the dimensions of partisan competition depart significantly from other regions, it has felt a powerful current sweeping away from one-party dominance (1970: 234).

As indicated in Figure 7.1, the presidential elections since the New Deal have indeed seen a narrowing of the gaps among the regions, with the Northeast no longer solidly Republican and the South less lopsidedly Democratic. And though not staggering in magnitude, Republican gains

FIGURE 7.1 Democratic Percentage of the Two-Party Presidential Vote, by Region.

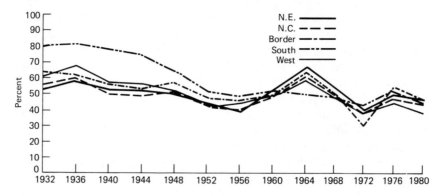

SOURCE: Ladd, 1970, p. 235, Fig. 5.7. Updates for 1972 and 1976 computed from data in *Statistical Abstracts of the United States: 1976* (Washington, D.C.: U.S. Bureau of the Census, 1976), and for 1980 from *Congressional Quarterly* (Weekly Report, 1981: 138).

in the South in the 1978 and the 1980 statewide and congressional races join with the presidential votes to imply further nationalization of two-party politics.[3]

That the melding of the regions may also be underway in Congress is less certain. Analysis of "North-South splits" reveals neither a pattern of rise *nor* decline in regional conflict in Congress over the past few decades; that measure, however, is computed across *all* Southern Democrats and may not be sensitive enough to the introduction of "new blood."[4] The power of incumbency in gaining reelection is well documented, and many of the congressmen who constitute today's Southern delegation were first elected to their positions before the South began its "transformation" from rural to industrialized and urban, a transformation which has seen the influx of many Northerners into Southern states. It is only as the more senior Southern congressmen are replaced that we will be able adequately to assess the change that may be taking place in Southern congressional politics.

Suggestive of the changes which *could* occur however, is a *Congressional Quarterly* study of the voting habits of the large group of freshmen representatives in the 94th Congress, of whom 18 were from Southern states. In both 1975 and 1976, the Southern Democratic freshmen gave their party somewhat more support than was the case for the non-freshmen Southerners.[5] Even more interesting than this finding, though, was one possible explanation for it. The freshman Democratic whip, himself from South Carolina, felt that the behavior witnessed in the 94th Congress would be more long-term than transitory; he told *Congressional Quarterly* (*Almanac*, 1975: 993, and *Weekly Report*, 1976: 212) that his Southern freshmen colleagues voted as they did because they "consider[ed] themselves more national in conscience and persuasion." If he was correct, such feelings could eventually result in a more cohesive congressional Democratic party. The fact that it is still too early to judge, in spite of the continuation of the '74 freshmen's behavior into 1977 and 1978, is evidenced in the behavior of the later "classes" of Southern freshmen who have not shown the added propensity to support the party.[6]

But if some *Southern* voters and congressmen have indeed considered themselves to be "more national in conscience and persuasion" recently, that is not the only region to be affected by such feelings. The focus of politics everywhere has seemingly shifted to national problems and to the need for national solutions to those problems. Since the new Deal, demands for equality of rights and services gradually replaced the cries for states' rights, which had played such a prominent role in earlier American politics. As civil rights and welfare state politics came to the fore, concurrent with technological "homogenization," attention shifted dramatically from local and regional to national interests. Michael Reagan has argued the point well:

My expectation in the broadest terms is that the fundamental trend in the development of our intergovernmental system will be a continued further development of the notion of a national community, and further continued ideological acceptance of the corollary proposition that it is proper for the goals and standards of public services to be set by the national government as a basis for uniform rights of citizens no matter where they live. . . . Equality before the law, as guaranteed by the Fourteenth Amendment, is confined in terms of that Amendment to certain specific kinds of discrimination; but by analogy, it is being extended broadly to equality of social services regardless of geographic location within the country. Combined with the general cultural homogenization occurring through the media of communications and the ease of transportation, this trend means the end of much of the social diversity that is the only logical basis for continuation of old style federalism in the sense of acceding to the different value norms of different geographic areas (1972: 155–156).

And so by this argument, not only have we witnessed a nationalization of *politics*, which by itself might contribute to party centralization, but also a nationalization of *polity power*, which could provide additional incentive for the parties to nationalize as well.[7]

Centralization of government. In our analyses, we have found support for the argument that decentralized polities tend to develop decentralized parties but that the federal form *alone* may not have the same effect. Given these findings, it would indeed be relevant to the American parties if their polity has become appreciably more centralized, *even if* the federal Constitution remains intact.

In *Federalist #45* we are given the following image of state dominance over the national level of government:

The State Government will have the advantage of the federal government, whether we compare them in respect to the immediate dependence of the one or the other; to the weight of personal influence which each side will possess; to the powers respectively vested in them; to the predilection and probable support of the people; to the disposition and faculty of resisting and frustrating the measures of each other (Washington Square Press edition, 1964: 99–100).

And while that might indeed have been an accurate picture of the relationship of the levels of government at the time of the nation's founding and even during its first century or so, it seems to be taken for granted today that the balance has shifted in favor of Washington. When asked in 1973 the degree to which the three levels of government affect people's lives, 63 percent of the respondents to a nationwide Harris survey indicated that the federal government affected their lives "a great deal," as opposed to only 39 percent for the state level and 38 percent for the local level.[8]

And the people's impressions are supported by Riker's analysis

(1964), in which he attempted to quantify his own impressions of the degree to which centralization (or decentralization) has occurred for 17 governmental functions. His conclusion: "the federal government has acquired more duties, in relation to the states, over the years; [b]oth kinds of governments have grown with the nation, but the federal government seems to have become somewhat more conspicuous than that of the states" (1964: 81).

None of this is meant to suggest that the states, as units of administration, have become obsolete or even unimportant. In fact, the state and local share of governmental expenditures has increased over time, not decreased (see Elazar, 1972: 57–59),[9] and likewise for the state and local share of total governmental employment.[10] But these are indicators of a continuing and growing *administrative* role for the lower levels of government, and they say very little about the extent to which these levels maintain *ultimate control* over the making of program decisions. So while the states may have an increasing role in administering policies, their share of governmental *power* (relative to the national level) may actually be declining.

While expenditures may be a good measure of governmental activity at a particular level and hence of its role in the administration of policies, a level's dependence on intergovernmental grants might be a better indicator of its ability to determine ultimately *how* the money is spent.

TABLE 7.1   The Growth of Federal Grants-in-Aid to State and Local Governments, 1950–1979

Fiscal year	Amount (millions)	Federal grants as a percent of	
		Total federal outlays	State-local expenditures
1950	$ 2,253	5.3	10.4
1960	7,020	7.6	14.7
1965	10,904	9.2	15.3
1970	24,018	12.2	19.4
1975	49,723	15.2	23.2
1979 (estimated)	85,020	17.0	26.2

SOURCE: Randall B. Ripley and Grace A. Franklin, *Congress, the Bureaucracy, and Public Policy.* (Homewood, IL: The Dorsey Press, 1980), p. 12.
ORIGINAL SOURCE: *Special Analyses, Budget of the United States Government, Fiscal Year 1979.* (Washington, D.C.: Government Printing Office, 1978), p. 184.

As evidenced in Table 7.1, the dependency of the lower levels upon national resources for their "expense accounts" has increased appreciably in recent years. Even though Congress has often *yielded* varying amounts of latitude in spending the grants, the facts remain that it was

Congress who originally established the grant, it was Congress who decided what strings should accompany it, it is Congress who decides whether to renew the grant, and it is Congress who will then decide whether more strings should be attached. And these conditions apply even to general revenue sharing, making the scheme more restrictive than is usually claimed.[11] And so, while the states and localities have come to depend upon the funds, ultimate control over their use has remained in Washington.

The implication of all of this for the parties is quite clear. Even though the constitutional structure of federalism has remained unchanged, the weakening of the *effective* decentralization of power would appear to have rendered another serious tear in the fabric of the parties' "decentralizing" environment.

Some centralizing "events". Whether resulting from the above trends or merely concurrent with them, some "events" of recent vintage have made the political environment even more receptive to the nationalization of party power. Both the Supreme Court and the Congress have recently helped to pave the way for the national parties to assume a heavier hand in their dealings with lower party organs.

The courts have for some time been involved in disputes arising from conflicts between party rules and state laws, and one case involving the Illinois delegation to the 1972 Democratic National Convention brought the matter to a head. The case involved a decision by the Convention to unseat a delegation selected under the laws of the state of Illinois, but by procedures ignoring the antidiscrimination guidelines of the party, and to replace it with another delegation selected separately under those guidelines. The issue, said the Supreme Court, was quite clear: Who wins in such disputes, the party or the state? Their conclusion:

> The convention serves the pervasive national interest in selection of candidates for national office, and this national interest is greater than any interest of an individual State. . . . Thus, Illinois' interest in protecting the integrity of its electoral process cannot be deemed compelling in the context of the selection of delegates to the National Party Convention [*Cousins v. Wigoda*, 95 S. Ct. 541 (1975)].

And in reaching that conclusion, the Court argued that:

> The vital business of the Convention is the nomination of the Party's candidates for the offices of President and Vice President of the United States. To that end, the state political parties are "affiliated with a national party through acceptance of the national call to send delegates to the national convention" [*Ray v. Blair*, 343 U.S. 214, 225 (1952)].

The decision undoubtedly went unnoticed by most of the public, but to students of political parties and to the parties themselves, the case was a milestone. The parties, denied even a mention in the Constitution, were now recognized as having precedence over even state law, at least in matters pertaining to the selection of delegates to the parties' conventions.[12] This recognition by the Court was reaffirmed in 1981 in its decision in *Democratic Party of the United States of America et al. v. LaFollette et al.*, which states the right of the national party to refuse convention seats to delegates selected in "open" primaries.

Though some would argue otherwise, the Congress may have provided a further boost to the national parties with the election reform legislation of the '70s. The *Federal Election Campaign Act*, as amended in 1974 and 1976, provides a significant role for the national parties by fully supporting both national conventions with public funds (to the tune of $2 million each) and allowing the parties themselves to provide a sizable chunk of campaign monies. The spending rules are rather complex and vary by the office and the committee involved. The national committees may contribute up to 2 cents per voter to the presidential general election campaign, which amounted to a maximum of $4.6 million in 1980. The national and congressional party committees may *each* give a maximum of $5,000 to a candidate in the primary and in the general elections. The national and senatorial party committees may contribute together a total of $17,500 to a Senate candidate. In addition to these direct expenditures, the national committees may make "coordinated" expenditures with the candidate's campaign. These spending ceilings are far higher: $14,720 for a House candidate and from $29,440 to $485,024 for a Senate candidate, depending on the state's population (Congressional Quarterly, *Weekly Report*, 1980: 3236).

It is true that the legislation could have strengthened the parties even more by making them (rather than campaign organizations) the recipients of public funds for campaigns. Nevertheless, the legislation directly altered the parties' political environment and allowed them to play an enlarged role in the election campaign. Citizens who wished to contribute more to a presidential candidate than the $1,000 allowed by the law could contribute $20,000 to the candidate's national party. The party could then distribute funds to state and local parties, which were allowed by a 1979 amendment to the Federal Election Campaign Act to purchase unlimited amounts of campaign materials to promote federal candidates and otherwise to promote the presidential candidate without counting it as a contribution against the spending limit. These features of the legal environment have helped to "institutionalize" the parties' campaign role (Congressional Quarterly, *Weekly Report*, 1980: 2011, and Congressional Quarterly, *Almanac*, 1979: 559–560). As *Congressional Quarterly* has interpreted the finance rules, "party organization enjoys a privileged spot" (*Weekly Report*, 1980: 3234).

A More "Receptive" Environment

The trends toward nationalization of issues, politics, and government, along with the events just mentioned, have combined to yield a *new* environmental configuration in the United States—one that is less conducive to extreme decentralization of party power. The spread of technological advances in transportation and communications have made this a *smaller* nation, "nationalizing" our thoughts about issues and problems and "centralizing" our approach to resolving those issues and problems. Even legislative cohesion may be more feasible now, the result of a natural "homogenization" of our society. Just as party discipline may now be necessary in order to take full advantage of the changed environment, a natural trend toward more cohesive voting (if such a trend should develop) could make the imposition of party discipline more acceptable.

While the transformation of the environment is an ongoing process and has hardly been completed, the wheels of these particular changes have already been turning for a long enough period to justify asking: Have the parties shown any inclination to take advantage of the changed environment? Have they made any moves in the direction of strengthening their national parties? There is evidence that at least the Democratic party has made some moves in the direction of placing more procedural control in the hands of the national organs. And though the Republicans have not rested greater procedural control at the national level of their party, the national organs have developed an impressive set of tools and functions that could potentially affect the relationships with their candidates and more local party organizations.

PARTY CHANGE IN THE '70s

In spite of the technologically induced homogenization, the nationalization of politics, and the centralization of polity power, the American parties were dramatic in their slowness to respond to the changed environment. In 1960, Rossiter put in this way:

> Although the direction of this country's course seems to be pointed steadily toward a great magnet located somewhere in Washington—with the result that we are moving fitfully but inexorably toward more centralized, nationalized, uniform ways of doing the public business—the organizational pattern of the two major parties has thus far resisted the lure of this magnet obstinately (1960: 12).

And as late as 1974, after noting the technological advances and associated trends that we have discussed here, Madron and Chelf were still able to conclude:

> At the same time that these tendencies are growing, our parties remain highly decentralized and locally oriented, and hence poorly equipped to cope with problems that are national in scope (1974: 332).

But recently, there have been some signs of new life in the national organs of both parties.

Change in the Democratic Party

Ranney argued in 1975 that recent attempts by the Democratic National Committee to sit in judgment on the qualifications of its members, by the party's national conventions to set standards by which selection of delegates is to be carried out, and by the party as a whole to provide itself with a written constitution all point to a "modest but distinct revival of national party control" (1975: 180–187). Five years later, Longley ventured that "a more authoritative national Democratic Party organization" had emerged from some of the recent reforms (1980a: 374).[13] Probably the most important single change, in that regard, was the creation of the party's first national charter less than a decade ago.

The Charter of the Democratic Party. In 1974, the Democrats held a midterm convention in Kansas City to do what no major American party in history had done—to write for itself a constitution. The meeting and its charge were of no small import for the party, as has been described by Crotty:

> Its intent was to revitalize and modernize structures that had evolved with little change since the late 1840's. The party, it was hoped, could be made relevant to the closing decades of the twentieth century. In the process, a subtle shift of power would occur: more authority would gravitate to the national party while at the same time the procedures of both the state and, more specifically, the federal party would be democratized (1977: 252).

Although the original expectations of some would-be reformers were not to be realized at the miniconvention, the resultant *Charter of the Democratic Party* did take some steps toward strengthening the national party.

As summarized by Crotty (and paraphrased by us; see Crotty, 1977: 253–5), the Charter did the following among other things:

1 Importuned the national party to take responsible positions on matters of policy that reflected the concerns of its supporters, a role it had attempted to fulfill through such agencies as the Democratic Advisory Council (1955–60) and the more recent Democratic Policy Council (1970) but one which some congressional and other party leaders felt it had no business playing.

2 *Allowed* for midterm party conferences to be held, with the time, place, agenda, and final decision of their being convened left in the hands of the National Committee.

3 Enforced the principles underlying the McGovern-Fraser and Mikulski Commissions' guidelines for delegate selection—indisputable evidence that these were permanent changes.

4 Established a Judicial Council to be appointed by the National Committee whose function "shall be to review and approve state plans for the selection of delegates to the National Conventions and to decide challenges to such state plans, provided, however, that the right of the Democratic National Convention and [the] Democratic National Committee to settle credentials disputes concerning their respective bodies shall not be abridged"—an innovative but somewhat more modest proposal than originally anticipated.

5 Created a National Finance Council to fund party affairs, the institutionalization of a vehicle that had been used in a more ad hoc fashion for several years (an approach the Republican party had employed with notable success).

6 Established a National Education and Training council to implement "education and training programs for the Democratic Party in furtherance of its objectives," a broad and unclear grant of authority to a new agency (responsible to the Executive Committee) roughly analogous to programs sponsored by the more centralized European democratic parties and one of the proposals for which the entire charter had been attacked for attempting to "Europeanize" the party.

7 Continued to recognize the National Convention as the supreme governing body of the party and required state parties to adapt their practices and rules to the national party standards and "to take provable positive steps" to change their state laws to conform to the charter and the National Convention directives should they conflict, an explicit and novel recognition of the national party's dominance.

8 Made all state parties adopt and file with the National Committee within 30 days of their ratification *written* rules for the conduct of all party business. This was a small point, but malleable and unspecified rules had long proven a source of great power to state party leaders.

9 Authorized the National Committee to "adopt and publish a code of fair campaign practices . . . *recommended* for observance by all candidates campaigning as Democrats" (emphasis added). (See Appendix B.)

Covering the areas of policy formulation, national leadership selection, fund raising and allocation, national influence on state and local organs, and communications, loosely defined, the Charter *would* affect many of the areas of decision making which are normally associated with national parties.[14] We emphasize *would* because, while some of the Charter's provisions have been implemented, it is still too early to tell whether the Charter's full potential will be realized.[15]

Nevertheless, we agree with Crotty that even the act of formulating the Charter was a monument to a new self-awareness of the national Democratic party:

> For the organizationally chaotic, decentralized, and unstructured American political parties, conditions especially true for the less organizationally astute Democratic party, the newly instituted party constitution signaled the beginning of a concerted drive to revivify the party. The intent was to make the party relevant to the demands of a technologically advanced society and an increasingly more sophisticated electorate. All of this was taking place at a time when political parties stood in disrepute and their future contributions to democratic society were suspect (1977: 255).

Though far less pervasive than the Charter, there are other indications of greater nationalization within the Democratic party.

Delegate selection. We have already noted the role which the national convention has come to play in establishing rules by which the next convention's delegates are to be selected. The mere fact of making such rules is not novel, but since 1972 it has become clear that the rules are actually enforceable. With the support of the Supreme Court's 1974 decision (*Cousins v. Wigoda*), it is clear that the national party has effectively appropriated what was for a long time considered to be a legitimate and nearly inviolable function of the state parties, the selection of *their* delegates to the national conventions. While it is true that the substance of the delegate selection rules of the early '70s were more "democratizing" than "strengthening," the party now appears to be somewhat more concerned with the latter. All delegate selection plans proposed by the state parties now require approval from the Democratic National Committee's Compliance Review Commission. And the most recent rules review commission (the "Winograd Commission," named for its chairman) recommended two rules intended to "curb the future growth of primaries and increase the influence of the party hierarchy," according to *Congressional Quarterly* (Elections '80: 68). The rules, which were first adopted by the Democratic National Committee in 1978, would (1) effectively shorten the primary season (beginning in 1984), thereby lessening the importance of early primaries, and (2) expand the size of the delegations and guarantee that the new seats would go to the state's party leaders and office holders. Following the 1980 elections, a number of Democratic notables proposed rule changes that would even further reduce the importance of primaries.[16]

Party finances. As we have already noted, the 1974 Charter established a national-level financial organ, but the long-range effect of that decision is yet to be seen. What has already been seen, however, is the impact of nationwide telethons, which raised millions of dollars between 1972 and 1975. Though the fund raisers were actually joint efforts of the national and state levels, a legal contract stated that "if there be any question or conflict in its interpretation, the sole decision as to whether or not a respective state qualifies for any proceeds shall rest with the DNC Chairman" (as cited in Longley, 1976: 17). As Longley has argued:

> Clearly, then, the supremacy of the federal level organization is manifested in a contractual document. And while the telethon was equally clearly a cooperative venture there can be little doubt that the preeminent role of the national organization was further enhanced and entrenched (1976: 17).

It can hardly be argued that the national level is now (or was during the 1972–75 period of the telethons) the primary collector and allocator of party funds, and it even appears that the telethon itself is now a thing of the past. Nevertheless, the telethon and the national level's role in it did establish a *precedent* for an improved position for the national organization vis-à-vis its affiliates. Whether the party can find the means to build on the precedent remains to be seen.

Legislative leadership and party discipline. The Democratic party in the Congress, especially in the House, has recently indicated a new willingness to give its leadership more power with which to lead and its caucus more tools with which to enforce its collective will. In the early and middle '70s, the House brought a number of reforms in its rules and procedures, including: (1) designating the Speaker as chair of a new Steering and Policy Committee designed to "help direct party strategy" (according to Dodd and Oppenheimer, 1981: 52), (2) transferring committee assignments to the Steering and Policy Committee, (3) giving the Speaker authority to nominate the Democratic members and chair of the Rules Committee, (4) providing for more regular meetings of the caucus, and (5) giving the caucus an effective role in choosing committee chairmen (possibly on grounds other than seniority).[17] According to Dodd and Oppenheimer (1981: 50), "to a degree [the reforms] reinvigorated the parties and presented them with new, expanded roles in the operation of the House." Though they add that the changes have "not thus far produced an institutionalized form of party government," there is no denying the importance of the recent changes in the House. Perhaps the most obvious effect already has been in the area of party discipline.

In 1975, the Democratic Caucus used its final approval of chairmanships to threaten removal of several powerful committee chairmen, and actually removed three. At the time, Hitlin and Jackson were quite correct in warning against overgeneralization:

> These removals in 1975 were based at least as much on grounds of age or

arbitrary and autocratic behavior as on policy grounds. It remains to be seen whether this power will develop into an instrument of accountability to enforce issue discipline, *although that potential at least exists now* (1975: 39; emphasis added).

That "potential" alone, though, could have an impact on the behavior of some legislators. "In the future" Hitlin and Jackson noted, "a chairman who is autocratic or unresponsive to the wishes of the Democratic Caucus will know that the caucus has exercised this removal power in the recent past (1975: 39)."

The potential became reality again in 1979, and although caution is still wise in interpreting the results, they may at least be additional evidence of a new attitude toward party discipline. Again, seniority was not strong enough to overcome the perceived "faults" of several candidates for subcommittee chairmanships, and three of them were passed over for more junior candidates.[18] The important difference between these cases and those in 1975, however, was the motive. "Instead of just challenging a senior member for autocratic behavior," *Congressional Quarterly* reported members as saying, "members were voting on whether one candidate's views are closer to theirs than the other's" (*Weekly Report*, 1979: 183). Since sanctions for ideological differences are the stuff of discipline, these recent events are especcially noteworthy.[19]

Also noteworthy is an action of the Democratic House Caucus in January 1981. When three Democratic members voted against the leadership's position on an organizational vote, the members were subsequently warned by the caucus to "toe the line" or face expulsion from the group, which would result in a loss of seniority.[20] This unusual forcefulness was taken as a sign that with its numbers depleted by the 1980 elections, the leadership and the caucus might be less reluctant to use discipline to maximize the effects of the fragile majority on parliamentary votes.

Some offsetting forces. Even with the Democratic party's important, recent attempts to develop some newly found muscles, it is still far from being "strong" at the national level today. Attempts have continued to further "democratize" the party, even at the expense of weakening it still more. As Ranney noted in 1975:

Since the late 1960s both major parties have tried to democratize their national conventions by increasing the influence of issue and candidate partisans over party regulars and officeholders (1975: 194).

The result has been to offset some of the moves toward strengthening the party.

Chief among the offsetting forces has been the dramatic increase in the use and importance of primary elections, which effectively remove the party's control over its most important and distinguishing function: the selection of its candidates. The number of primaries has grown from 17 in 1968, to 23 in 1972, to 30 in 1976, and to a record 37 in 1980 (according to Congressional Quarterly, *Elections '80*: 68). Now, finally, there seems to be a growing awareness of the price that the parties are paying for yielding the nominating decisions to primary voters (who in some cases do not even have to be party identifiers). *Congressional Quarterly* has noted the new attitude:

> Many party leaders are beginning to feel the growth in primaries has gone too far, creating a nominating system that emphasizes candidates' personal campaign organizations and media advertising while relegating the national, state and local party leadership to a back seat (*Elections '80*: 68).

Although adoption of the Winograd Commission's recommendations may help to turn the tide, it will not be an easy process to change the "open party" habits that seemed to develop their own momentum. If the increasing role for primaries is to be stopped, it will most likely occur in the next quadrennium as a "practical" response to what some Democrats now see as a factor in the party's dismal record in the 1980 elections.[21]

Before making a final assessment of what could be a "nationalizing trend" within the Democratic party, we first turn to the recent changes that have taken place in the Republican party.

Change in the Republican Party

Recent changes in the Republican party have been much less controversial (and thus less visible) than those of the Democrats, but they have also been significant, though quite different in character. Bibby argues that, while the Democrats were engaging in *procedural* reform, the Republicans were conducting *organizational* reform. The difference corresponds closely to that between the concepts of decentralization and organizational complexity. Reforms in the Democratic party were aimed at "vesting legal authority over presidential nominating processes with the national committee," whereas in the Republican party they involved "performing or supplementing the organizational and campaign functions previously considered to be the domain of state and local party and candidate committees" (1980: 113–114). In short, the Democrats sought to centralize authority within the national committee; the Republicans sought to develop the capacity of the national committee to help state and local parties and candidates win elections.

Republicans have traditionally placed a greater value on organizational details than Democrats. The rules governing the Republican National Committee and the Republican National Convention (see Appendix C) were more carefully codified than the "common law" that governed the Democratic party before the adoption of its charter in 1974 (Bibby, 1980: 103). This regard for formalization, however, did not extend to centralization. Responding to the Democrats' efforts at self-evaluation following the 1968 and 1972 conventions, the Republicans created two reform committees. The 1969 Committee on Delegates and Organization (known as the "DO Committee") recommended electing more minority delegates to the party convention but stopped far short of setting mandatory quotas for state parties. The Rule 29 Committee, appointed in 1973, did recommend that state parties file reports on their minority action programs with the national committee but did not grant the committee any powers of enforcement. Even this weak proposal for centralization was defeated by the national committee itself and re-nounced by the Republican National Convention in 1976 (Bibby, 1980: 105). The Convention proceeded to adopt rules that recognized state party rights in delegate selection. These rules were reaffirmed by the 1980 Convention. As noted by *Congressional Quarterly*:

> Unlike the Democrats, Republicans have neither a compliance review com-mission nor detailed requirements to which states must adhere .... Except for basic guidelines, nearly all important decisions are left to the state par-ties or to state law (*Elections '80*: 70–71).

Lost in the controversy over the Rule 29 Committee's "positive action" program for increasing minority representation in delegate selection were its other recommendations for reforming the party structure, which *were* accepted by the 1976 Convention (and were reaffirmed in 1980). As summarized by Bibby, they provided that:

(1) the chairman and cochairman shall be full-time paid employees of the Republican National Committee;

(2) there shall be eight vice chairmen, consisting of one man and woman elected from each of four regions;

(3) the term of office of the Republican National Committee officers shall be two years (thereby giving the Republican National Committee for-mal power to pass judgment on its chairman and officers every two years);

(4) the composition of the Executive Committee shall be specified (thereby limiting the appointing discretion of the chairman);

(5) the Republican National Committee shall confirm the chairman's appointment of the General Counsel;

(6) the powers of the Executive Committee shall be specified, and the chairman shall be required to call at least four meetings of the commit-tee annually;

(7) Republican National Committee approval of the budget shall be re-quired; and

(8) the chairman shall be required to send out in advance of Republican National Committee meetings [an] agenda, minutes, and the proposed budget (1980: 105). (See Appendix C: Rules 25, 26, 27, and 28.)

These recommendations were aimed at restructuring the Republican National Committee (RNC) in keeping with the idea of organizational reform, i.e., improving the committee's services to its sovereign state parties. Ben Cotten, former director of the RNC's Division of Political Affairs, believes that the 1976 rule establishing the chairman and cochairman as full-time paid positions was one of the most significant changes in the party but one that was often overlooked by party scholars (Cotten, 1981). He also argues that the organizational realignment of the national committee was largely successful because of the efforts of the RNC's first full-time chairman, Bill Brock. Brock's role in rebuilding the party has been widely recognized (*National Journal*, 1980: 1617).

The Republican party had always been more organizationally developed than the Democratic party, and its research division had long been more active than the Democrats'.[22] Under Brock's chairmanship, the RNC increased its research and service capacity. It acquired its own computer in 1977 and upgraded to a newer one in 1979. The party increased its existing publication program, publishing a variety of magazines, reports, and newsletters. *Commonsense*, a journal of thought and opinion, and *Public Opinion Report*, a weekly summary of poll data on political topics, are noteworthy recent additions. For the 1980 campaign, the RNC had 390 employees housed in its own four-story building off Capitol Hill—compared to the 80 employees of the Democratic National Committee (DNC) occupying a floor of the Airline Pilot's Association building in downtown Washington (Cotten, 1981, and *National Journal*, 1980: 1618).

More importantly, the RNC under Brock applied its organizational capacity to develop and implement several new programs for assisting Republican candidates that overshadowed any comparable efforts by the Democratic National Committee. The RNC created a Local Elections Campaign Division (LECD) in 1978 to direct a national effort at winning seats in state legislatures. Bibby reports:

> In conjunction with state party organizations, the LECD collected data on thousands of districts, developed district profiles, and helped state organizations identify target districts.... From January to September 1978, the LECD sponsored 75 candidate seminars. In the eastern region alone, out of 4,100 legislative districts, the campaigns of approximately 2,700 candidates were represented at one of the LECD seminars (1980: 110).

This unprecedented activity by an American national party appeared to pay off in the 1978 elections; the national party liked the result, and the program was expanded in 1980.[23] Ninety-six seminars trained more than 5000 candidates and their staffs (Cotten, 1981).[24]

The RNC also began a program of financial support and staff direction to the Republican Governors' Association in 1978, establishing a task force for state campaigns that visited 12 states to provide evaluations and advice concerning campaign plans and headquarters operations[25] (Bibby, 1980: 111–112). The RNC was equally active in campaigns for the United States Congress. It gave $1.1 million to 138 Republican candidates for the House and showed a gain of 33 seats. It spent nearly $.4 million for Senate contests and picked up 12 seats and control of the Senate for the first time since 1954 (Republican National Committee, 1981).

The magnitude of the Republican national organization's campaign activities can be compared with that of the Democrats by reference to the astounding difference in expenditures reported in Table 7.2. According to data furnished by the Federal Election Commission, the national, congressional, and senatorial committees of the Republican party outspent the counterpart committees of the Democrats by more than $100 million—a ratio of over 6 to 1!

TABLE 7.2   Expenditures by Democratic and Republican National Party Organizations in the 1980 Elections[a]

	Democratic	Republican
National Committees	$14,909,724	$ 71,013,779
Congressional Committees	2,038,401	25,690,935
Senatorial Committees	1,618,162	21,920,337
Totals	$18,566,287	$118,625,051

[a] SOURCE: Federal Election Commission, Index C, dated February 24, 1981. These data are the total expenditures disclosed from January 1, 1979, through December 30, 1980.

So far, these organizational and financial efforts by the Republicans have occurred without insistence on national direction and control. While the Democrats have attempted to achieve more procedural control through their national organs, the Republicans have been content to mold something akin to a national service bureau. It appears that the party has extended its philosophy of *governmental* decentralization to *party* decentralization. Crotty explains:

> The Republicans, during the post-World War II period, and as the Democrats were forced into a more activist role nationally in supervising local and state parties particularly in relation to racial excesses, had become perhaps more politically committed to the ideological implications of a highly decentralized party system. Authority over state matters such as delegate selection standards resided at the lower levels. This emphasis did not prohibit a strong national headquarters staff from emerging, but it did require that the national party assure a basically supportive and supplemental posture to state party actions. Noninterference was emphasized. Power, if not always political resources, remained at the state level. Within this framework, any reform recommendations that impinged on what were considered state processes, even if adopted by the national convention, were accepted only as suggestions (1977: 256).

Although the Republicans continue to heed their aversion to national control of state and local party activities, the national organization has become such an important source of funds and intelligence for candidates at all levels that one wonders how long organizational reform (i.e., greater complexity) can exist without procedural reform (i.e., centralization). For example, Cotten notes that in the past, the RNC financed part of its activities by assessing the state parties a certain quota for national operations. As a result of the Federal Election Campaign Act and new programs for fund raising in the RNC, the national organization became "a distributor of funds not only to candidates but to state parties rather than merely a collector of funds" (1981). If the RNC pays the piper, the RNC may decide to call the tune.

Although the potential for power exists in the Republican National Committee, there are two factors which may halt its exercise. One is the Republican aversion to national control. The other, ironically, is the party's success in winning the Presidency in 1980. As Bibby writes:

> The ultimate test of the durability of Republican National Committee programs is likely to come when the GOP next regains the presidency and the Republican National Committee ceases to be the most important and inclusive Republican organization in the country (1980: 114).

American Presidents have not looked with favor on strong national party organizations, *especially* in their own parties. If President Reagan bucks the pattern and encourages the national Republican organization, the party could write a new chapter in American electoral and legislative politics. But if he does not and follows the path of President Kennedy, who relegated an invigorated DNC to a minor role after he won office following eight years of Republican government, the RNC could lose its momentum.

The Net Result: A *Stronger* Party System?

The picture of recent party reform toward stronger national parties is one of slow procedural change in the Democratic party and reluctance on the part of the national Republican party to use its increased organizational prowess to its full potential as a lever of internal party control. That these changes have not yet dramatically increased the "power" of the national parties should probably not surprise us. It may be true that signs of change in the environment have been apparent for at least two decades, but habits of decentralization and "democratization" that have been learned over half a century could not be immediately forgotten or replaced.

Advocates of stronger parties should be encouraged by signs that at least the Democratic party has *finally* begun the process of procedural change that may lead to strengthening the national party. And although the Republican party may not have engaged in *that* process yet, additional encouragement might be found in the fact that the Republican party has now acquired some of the organizational resources which could be converted into a stronger role vis-a-vis the other party organs, should the party choose to move in that direction.

Indeed, if we could stop here, we might sign off with a rather positive statement on the future of the American parties, a statement that would be pleasing to at least the proponents of stronger and more programmatic parties for this country. We have suggested that even stronger national institutions may be welcome in the changed American environment; in fact, the traditionally weak national parties may be ill-suited to the more "nationalized" government and politics. In that light, it might appear that the prospects for the American parties are quite bright— that they are likely to continue in a place of prominence on the changing American political landscape, *if only* they continue to strengthen themselves.

But we must view the parties in yet another light. To stop here would be to ignore other environmental changes—changes that could threaten the very existence of the American parties. Though nationalization of the parties may be a necessary component of a successful party scenario for the future, it may not be a sufficient condition. Mass parties of *any* kind may be put to the test in this new political environment. The party changes which have just been documented could yet prove to be "too little and too late."

NOTES

1. See Gelb and Palley (1975) for a discussion of America's antiparty tradition.

2. As reported in Ranney (1975: 53–54), a 1969 *Newsweek* poll (29 December 1969, p. 43) found parties to rank below universities, business, organized religion, and police.

3. In 1978 the Republicans had a net gain of four House seats and one governorship *Congressional Quarterly* (*Weekly Report*, 1978: 3291) interpreted the results as "a few signs that the Republican Party might be able to grow in the South if it tries again." The largest moral victories came in Texas (first Republican governor in over 100 years) and Mississippi (first popularly elected Republican senator). In 1980, the Republican party had net gains of nine House seats, four Senate seats, and one governorship in Southern states (Congressional Quarterly, *Weekly Report*, 1980: 3302, 3319, and 3327). Louisiana's governorship went to the GOP in 1979.

4. *Congressional Quarterly* defines a North-South split as a recorded vote where a majority of Southern Democrats oppose a majority of Northern Democrats. The history of North-South splits from 1960 to 1976 is reported in the

1976 *Almanac*, p. 1014. Later data are provided in the 1977 *Almanac*, p. 39-B, and in the *Weekly Report*, 1978, p. 3480.

5. According to *Congressional Quarterly* (*Almanac*, 1975: 994), the average "party unity" score for Southern Democratic freshmen in 1975 was 55%, as compared to 47% for their nonfreshmen counterparts. The respective figures for 1976 (as reported in the *Almanac*, 1976: 1018) were 51% and 44%.

6. All 18 Southern members of the House's "class of '74" were reelected in 1976. Their average level of support in 1977 was 55%, as compared to 50% for more senior Southern members. In 1978, the proportions were 50% and 45%, respectively. However, later freshmen classes of Southern Democrats actually provided slightly *less* support to their party than the more senior group. The 14 Southern freshmen in the "class of '76" produced average support scores of 50% in 1977 and 41% in 1978, as compared to 51% and 47% respectively for their nonfreshman counterparts (computed from data in Congressional Quarterly, *Almanac*, 1977: 36B–37B, and *Almanac*. 1978: 32C–33C). The 17 Southern Democratic freshmen in the "class of '78" produced average party unity scores of 52% in 1979 and 54% in 1980, as compared to 56% and 58% respectively for Southern Democratic nonfreshmen (computed from data in Congressional Quarterly, *Almanac*, 1979: 32C–33C, and *Weekly Report*, 1981: 82–83).

7. It is testimony to the prevalence with which this view was held in early 1981 that it was considered by all major networks and wire services to be newsworthy when newly appointed Budget Director David Stockman stated on ABC's "Issues and Answers" that "I just don't accept the assumption that the federal goverment has a responsibility to supplement the income of the working poor through a whole series of transfer payments" (as reported in Congressional Quarterly, *Weekly Report*, 1981: 668) and that the administration even found it necessary to state and defend this challenge to the idea of nationally guaranteed "social rights."

8. Louis Harris and Associates conducted the survey of 1596 respondents in September 1973 under commission from the U.S. Senate Subcommittee on Intergovernmental Relations. The results were published in *Confidence and Concern: Citizens View American Government* (Regal Books/Kings Court Communications, 1974).

9. See also Dahl (1981), pp. 167–168, and especially Table 12.1, which shows that state and local expenditures have increased at approximately the same rate as federal expenditures on "civil functions" over time.

10. See, for instance, the Advisory Commission on Intergovernmental Relations' *American Federalism: Into the Third Century* (Washington, D.C.: 1974), p. 4.

11. Though revenue sharing may have been envisioned as a no-strings-attached means of returning revenues to the more local levels, it must be noted that: (1) the program is not permanent, and in fact is renewed at the pleasure of Congress; (2) the no-strings-attached concept does not apply to an antidiscrimination clause which has effectively held up the dispersal of some funds; and (3) the funds are not being "returned" to the states and localities according to their contributions, but according to their needs.

In other words, another way of viewing this "decentralization" program is as a *national* program of redistributing the wealth. That the program is not permanent and that the states have become dependent on the funds were both demonstrated when the 96th Congress cut the states out of the program for fiscal 1981. Even though the 1980 law does allow for states to reenter the program in fiscal 1982–3, such reentry would be conditional on the states' giving up an equal amount of categorical grants. (See Congressional Quarterly, *Weekly Report*, 1980: 3628.)

12. For an excellent accounting of this incident at the 1972 convention and its ramifications for the party, see Crotty (1976). The party continues to dictate delegate selection procedures to the state level; for 1980 it required state delegations to be equally divided between men and women and did not allow winner-take-all primaries of the single-member-district variety. Other winner-take-all primaries were outlawed earlier.

13. Indeed, some scholars attribute so much importance to the recent changes that the now familiar descriptions of "wrecking," "dismantling," and "decline" of American parties (Ladd, 1977; Kirkpatrick, 1978; and Crotty and Jacobson, 1980) have recently been joined by talk of "party renewal" (Pomper, 1980). Longley, who has gone so far as to herald a "transformation" of the national party organizations (1980b: 84), is correct in warning, though, that "to overstate the case would be just as much an error as to ignore the changes that have occurred" (1980a: 375).

14. The five areas of decision making referred to here are five of the seven included in an earlier cross-national study (Harmel, 1977 and 1978). The remaining two, discipline in the legislature and nomination of legislative candidates, are not directly affected by the Charter's provisions.

15. Even the future of miniconventions is still in doubt. It was generally felt that the likelihood of a convention in 1982 would have been lessened by the election of a Democratic President in 1980. The 1978 convention indicated to some that a midterm convention during a Democratic Presidency serves an uncertain purpose and that the institution cannot survive if its major purpose is to rubber-stamp the program of an incumbent President. Nevertheless, the 1980 National Convention did call for a mid-term conference, and in 1981 the Democratic National Committee "took a major step away from the participatory politics of the 1970s when it voted to shrink the size of the 1982 mid-term party convention almost by half and allocate most of the delegate seats to elected and party officials" (David Broder, "DNC Tightens its Grip on Setting Party Policies," *Houston Chronicle*, 6 June 1981, Sec. 1, p. 12).

16. For instance, Senator Alan Cranston of California proposed a plan whereby no more than a third of the delegates to the national convention would be chosen in binding primaries. (See "Dems May Lessen Importance of Primaries," *Houston Chronicle*, 4 February 1981, editorial page.) Former Secretary of State Cyrus Vance, writing in *The New York Times Magazine* ("Reforming the Electoral Reforms," 22 February 1981, pp. 16, 62–69), indicated finding considerable merit in the idea of "attempt[ing] to restore a balance between direct selection of a candidate by voters in primaries and selection by party and Congressional leaders."

17. For a more complete discussion of the changes, see Dodd and Oppenheimer (1981), pp. 51–55.

18. Specifically, the more junior subcommittee chairmen in the 96th Congress were Henry Waxman, who was elected chairman of the Commerce Health Subcommittee over Richard Preyer; Bob Ecklund, who defeated John Murphy

for the Oversight and Investigation Subcommittee; and Toby Moffett, who won the Environment, Energy, and Natural Resources chairmanship over three more senior candidates (Congressional Quarterly *Weekly Report*, 1979: 183). In 1981 no committee chairmanships went to anyone other than the ranking Democrat, though there was a challenge to Rep. Eligio de la Garza as chairman of the Agriculture Committee. De la Garza won by a slim margin, 110 to 92. (Cragg Hines, "Texan Barely Wins House Agriculture Position," *Houston Chronicle*, 12 December 1980, sec. 1, p. 20). Another serious challenge was made to Rep. Henry Gonzalez as chairman of the Banking Committee's Housing and Community Development Subcommittee (Congressional Quarterly, *Weekly Report*, 1981: 283). Both challenges were made on the basis of perceived qualifications of the more senior candidates.

19. In recent years there have been a large number of reforms in the party apparati in Congress which have suggested to some Congress watchers that we could see a renewal of party leadership within the national legislature. For a discussion of several rules changes and their potential impact on the parties (and especially the Democratic party) in Congress, see Dodd and Oppenheimer's "The House in Transition: Change and Consolidation" in their *Congress Reconsidered* (1981). See especially the section entitled "Strengthening Party Leadership" on pages 50–59.

20. Cragg Hines, "Dems Vote Party Line on Assignments," *Houston Chronicle*, 29 January 1981, sec. 1, p. 11.

21. See note 16.

22. A study of the sizes of the paid staff of both national committees from 1952 to 1977 shows that the Republican National Committee averaged 204 employees to the Democratic National Committee's 132 (Cotter and Bibby, 1980). The Republican party has published detailed analyses of election results since at least 1960 (Republican National Committee, 1961). Since 1964 it has also operated a unique microfilm information retrieval system for newspaper clippings. The system uses Eastman Kodak's MIRACODE equipment and is used mainly for "opposition" research, i.e., to search previously indexed newspaper clippings for statements by Democratic candidates and officials on public policy and political affairs.

23. Though it would be folly to point to the Republican organizational changes as the explanation for the victories, the increased activity undoubtedly contributed to those successes. The party had lost 692 seats in state houses across the nation in 1974, following President Nixon's resignation over the Watergate affair. In 1976, without the LECD activity, the party netted a gain of only 12 seats. In 1978, following the LECD activity, the party gained 307 seats (*First Monday*, December–January, 1981: 14–15).

24. This increased activity was accompanied by another gain of 271 state legislators (*First Monday*, December–January, 1981: 15). Lest one think that the gain was due to more than Reagan's victory with 51% of the presidential vote, one should note that the party won only 101 state seats nationwide in 1972, when President Nixon was reelected with 61%.

25. It should be noted that this effort was expended on a year when the party gained 7 governorships for a total of 19. In 1980 the RNC expanded its support to the Republican Governors' Association, giving $500,000 for races in 13 states. The party picked up 4 more governorships for a total of 23.

8

The Still-Changing Environment: Dimensions Affecting the Role of Parties

Along with the American environment's "centralizing" changes discussed earlier, the advanced stages of industrialization (or "postindustrialism") have also brought environmental changes that may be *threatening* to the very existence of political parties. Roles that have traditionally been performed by parties are now shared with mass media and thousands of interest groups. Even the *issues* over which the parties have done battle for decades were muted in a period of general affluence—and may be replaced by issues less easily managed by mass political parties.

POTENTIAL THREATS TO PARTIES

New Issues

An impressive literature exists to document the fact that major partisan "realignments" have occurred in this country about every 36 years and that these realignments have accompanied significant changes in what are perceived as the major political issues (or problems) affecting the country.[1] It is generally accepted that one such transformation of the party system occurred when the Great Depression caused economic regulation to be supplanted by welfare state issues as the major focus of public attention and Roosevelt responded by forging his New Deal coalition. Ever since the 1930s, FDR's party has been doing battle with the Republican party primarily over welfare-related issues. There have, of course, been other issues, too (e.g., anticommunism and civil rights), but none have been seen as defining the differences between the two parties as clearly as welfare policies.

If the pattern of 36-year renewals were to continue, a realignment should have occurred in or around 1968. And while the preponderance of evidence suggests that the anticipated realignment of voters has not occurred, it could be argued that the change in issues, or at least the addition of new issues, arrived right on schedule. Although we can hardly target 1968 as *the* turning point, it does appear that Americans' collective attentions have again turned in new directions.

With postindustrialism came a period of affluence that has had a profound influence on the lives of the bulk of Americans. Even though it could hardly be claimed that poverty has been eliminated, the fact is that much of the working class has moved from lower-class to middle-class status and that the problems of the poor are now personally felt by the few rather than the many.[2] And as the many have become more comfortable, they have found it somewhat less noxious to share through public programs. By the '70s, Americans seemed to have settled on a solution to the problems of the '30s and '40s—a modified free enterprise system with a moderate dosage of social welfare Even in the 1980 presidential campaign, which did focus attention on critical economic problems and budget and tax cuts as a possible solution to those problems, continuation of most of the basic social welfare programs was never seriously in doubt.[3]

With postindustrialism and affluence, however, came other problems (or at least the *awareness* of other problems) and issues. They include "quality of life" issues such as the environment[4] and more focused attention on such issues as equal rights for women, gun control, and abortion. But while such issues had come to dominate political discussion by the 1970s (along with current economic problems, of course), they did not replace welfare issues as the central focus of inter*party* debate.

If "realignment" was replaced by "dealignment" in the '70s, one reason may have been the apparent inability of the parties to provide meaningful choices of these "new" issues. We have already suggested that part of the problem may lie with the parties themselves: their weak and incohesive natures make them generally inefficient in dealing with problems defined as national in scope. But another reason may lie outside the parties' control; the issues themselves may not be well suited to mass party politics as we have known it. If a realignment is to occur to "reinvigorate" the party system, then attention must be shifted to new issues *which the parties can manage and on which they can provide meaningful choices.*

Issues that are too narrow. In considering which of the "new" issues might serve as the basis of a mass, long-term realignment, several must be dismissed as lacking sufficient salience for the broad range of American voters. With the public generally assuming that the "biggest" social problems were either being taken care of or had already been largely resolved, attention in recent years could be turned to "narrower" issues. With the knowledge (or at least *belief*) that the social welfare was provided for, the "Red menace" in check, and the major civil rights battles behind them, Americans could tend to (and could demand media attention for) other issues. Abortion, gun control, the Equal Rights Amendment, and legalization of marijuana are just a few examples. While each of these may be the *most* important concern for a small segment of Americans, none of these issues would generate (or at least none has generated) the kind of mass salience necessary to serve as the basis of a prolonged, mass partisan alignment. In short, they are not the basic "stuff" of mass party politics.

Such issues have become the turf of "single-issue" campaigns and "single-issue" interest groups. Groups such as the Right to Life Committee and Stop ERA do not require support from a plurality of the electorate; they are better suited than parties to articulating the views of their relatively small but extremely intense clienteles. For years, neither party saw fit to take a strong position on the abortion issue; it was perceived as the type of moral position that would cost a party far more support than it could gain. It was not until 1980, after right-to-life groups had demonstrated that the issue could actually be used to the political benefit of conservative candidates, that the Republican party saw fit to take a clear anti-abortion position in its platform.[5] And it was also not until 1980, with pro-ERA forces perceived to have lost their initial momentum, that the Republican convention broke with *both* parties' pattern of endorsing the ERA. Even then, the Republican presidential candidate stressed that he opposed not the *goal* of the amendment, but only the amendment *per se*.

Although the Republicans sought to "partyize" these issues in 1980 and undoubtedly gained some votes (and probably lost others) because of them, they were neither the major issues of the campaign (the economy and "management" were certainly among the more important) nor the deciding factors for most voters. Nor are these issues or the others like them likely to generate the type of mass interest necessary to cause a realignment in the future. They are likely to remain only secondary issues in political party politics and to continue as the primary causes for the organization of single-minded interest groups.

Issues that require priorities. Some of the broader issues that are high on today's public agenda are ill-suited to mass party politics for another reason: they require the setting of priorities, and that kind of politics may be too "messy," or at least unpleasant, for most voters. Politics organized around states' rights, regulation of the economy, and even social welfare programs may seem straightforward in comparison: voters might "want" or "not want" such things. But many political choices are not at all simple today. We *all* want a clean environment, for instance, but we *all* want to solve the energy problem as well. We all want full employment, but all want to beat inflation as well. . . .[6]

A realignment based on priorities—with one party giving a higher priority to the environment and the other to energy, with one determined to solve inflation first and the other unemployment—would be difficult to achieve for at least two reasons. First, Americans themselves are not inclined toward prioritizing—such choices are more difficult than most voters would care to contend with. "Wanting" or "not wanting" is just far simpler than being forced to "choose" between two valued goods or services. Those who today are warning that growth cannot continue unchecked, and hence that difficult choices must be made, are well aware that one consequence of decades of affluence is a lack of education in the act of choosing. Second, it is much too easy for the party "in power" to usurp the other party's position; witness the 1976 Carter *campaign's* intention to solve unemployment first but the *administration's* later decision that solving inflation should be given the higher priority. It is difficult to imagine a long-term partisan alignment based on issues where parties can so easily slide up and down the "priority scale."

Issues that require technical solutions. A third category of issues (actually encompassing some of those already mentioned) requires technical expertise in order to make an informed choice. A new alignment might split those favoring a "coal" solution to the energy shortage from those favoring an "oil" or "nuclear" solution. But the American public is ill-equipped to deal with such issues, and so are mass parties.

Interest groups already exist to represent the positions of those who have (or at least claim to have) the technical expertise required to make informed decisions on such issues. Interest groups do not require a mass clientele and hence need not be concerned that the bulk of American citizens neither have the requisite knowledge nor particularly want it.

Old and new issues: a summary. Some might suggest that the 1980 elections are evidence that the joint plagues of inflation and recession have breathed new life into the *old* issues—that the victory of Ronald Reagan signified a willingness on the part of a large segment of the voting public to "withdraw" from the modified welfare state that had seemingly become a nonissue. If such were the case, then perhaps the party system would be rejuvenated by the new vitality of the "old" issues. We feel that such a conclusion would be premature at best. First, the discussion of welfare issues during the 1980 presidential campaign concentrated on the "margins" of the welfare structure; both candidates pledged that many of the *basic* social programs would not be dismantled.[7] Second, there is evidence that popular support for welfare programs remains relatively intact, in spite of a willingness to see the budget pared.[8] And third, the Reagan victory itself would seem to be more a sign of disaffection with the management skills of the Carter Administration than of genuine disaffection with "liberal" programs.[9]

If this assessment is correct, it would seem to suggest something quite different from a reinvigoration of the "old" issues. It could even portend more elections where management skills of candidates, rather than issues of parties, would dominate national elections.

"New" issues would seem to offer little more hope for revitalizing the party system. The kinds of issues discussed above, and particularly those of the latter two categories, are the types of issues that might be expected to arise in an age of postindustrialism. They are issues that require especially difficult choices and a large amount of technical knowledge in order to make informed decisions.

The new issues would appear to be ill-suited to politics organized by political parties, and some of them appear ill-suited to politics by the masses. We are not the first to suggest that postindustrialism could bring a politics of technocrats.[10] We are also not the first to point out that interest groups are waiting in the wings to organize the "new" politics.

Interest Groups

President Carter's aide for liaison with interest groups, Ann Wexler, estimated in 1978 that there were already 6000 of them operating in Washington.[11] While some of these groups have long histories of articulating their clienteles' special desires and concerns to the government and of "educating" the public in hopes of generating more general support for their positions, many more have arisen in just the past few decades. The National Right to Life Committee (favoring a "human life" amendment) and the Religious Coalition for Abortion Rights (opposing such an amendment), the National Organization for Women (favoring the ERA) and Stop ERA (opposing it), the American Nuclear Energy Council (promoting nuclear energy) and the Environmental Coalition on Nuclear Power (opposing it) exemplify the new forces evident in interest group politics. As we have already noted, many issues on today's national agenda seem somewhat better suited to articulation by interest groups than by parties. For that reason and because modern technology makes the groups' "educational" function more effective and efficient, there has been a proliferation of interest groups and a concomitant rise in their collective importance.

Despite limitations placed on PAC (political action committee) campaign contributions by the Federal Election Campaign Act, political action committees contributed in excess of $55 million to congressional campaigns in 1980 (compared to about $12 million by the parties), with "conservative" interest groups alone contributing more than $13 million.[12] As Crotty and Jacobson argue, the significant role given to political action committees in funding campaigns and "the modern campaign technology have encouraged the emergence of new single-interest groups (on abortion, the gun lobby, Proposition 13) and ideological interest groups that have an increasing impact on the parties, the conduct of campaigns, and the nature and policy commitments of elected public officials" (1980: 65). Whether interest groups alone could ever be a *satisfactory* replacement for parties or not (and we will say more on that later), the fact remains that for some kinds of issues, they are the most effective participants (or the *only* participants) in the battles today. Bolstered by the impression of growing influence in Washington, claims of enviable election success records by such groups as the Right to Life Committee and NCPAC (National Conservative Political Action Committee),[13] and a consequent rise in media attention, interest group politics has become a formidable rival to party politics today.

Mass Media

Just as articulation is one traditional party function that is now being performed by interest groups, two other "party functions," setting the national agenda and educating voters on issues and candidates, are now performed by the mass media. Postindustrialism is an age of rapid and, for the consumer, relatively inexpensive communications. The political effects of "a television in every living room" have been felt in many ways, and campaigning is no exception. According to Crotty and Jacobson:

> Television is the new political god. It has supplanted the political party as the main conduit between candidate and voter (1980: 67).

Television is simply a much "cheaper" means of obtaining political information than reading campaign fliers or attending political rallies.

The effects on agenda setting are no less pronounced. Where parties were once perceived as the major source (or at least *a* major source) of the nation's "program" and priorities, the media, both directly and through its polls, have largely usurped that role. As Ladd and Hadley have noted concerning the modern mass media:

> Its decisive resource is control of the political agenda, influence over how problems are conceptualized, which are deemed to have the highest priority, what responses are worthy of credence, and which merit only rejection (1978: 190–191).

And if these direct effects of the media on the parties' roles were not enough, there are also important indirect effects. Again as Ladd and Hadley (1978: 380) have noted, "The national media are candidate- and issue-emphasizing vehicles, not party emphasizing." While parties have undoubtedly been able to take some advantage of the new media, it would appear that those same media have also made parties somewhat more dispensable. The 1980 presidential campaign of independent candidate John Anderson (without so much as a third-party label) is testimony to both the importance of media exposure and the declining importance of the party label.

Summary: A Non-Party Environment?

The age of postindustrialism has affected American politics in many important ways. Mass communications and rapid transportation have contributed to an homogenization of our thinking about politics, resulting in a more "national" political focus. The new technologies, as well as the new issues that have come with them, have also resulted in (1) a more efficient means of conveying and receiving political information that has made parties largely irrelevant to the task and (2) a politics that may be more suited to interest groups than to today's parties.

It is possible, and certainly ironic, that the same period of environmental change that has made strengthening of the American parties more feasible may also have made those parties unnecessary and perhaps even obsolete. If it has ever been important for the parties to consider major reform, it would seem that it is even more important today. Though the parties have already effected several changes in the direction of stronger or more active national organizations, they still appear ill-equipped to deal with the challenges that lie ahead. The parties face an uncertain future, and with them so does American politics, not so unlike the uncertainty of American politics at our founding.

SOME FINAL THOUGHTS

American Parties: The First on the Landscape

It is perhaps too easy to forget that there have not always been parties, and hence just to *assume* that there will always be parties. But even in democracies, there have not always been parties; democracy, after all, preceded America, and our Constitution preceded the development of the first "modern" political parties. So before considering what politics might be like in an America without parties and what might be developed to replace them, it may be enlightening to review the situation in which parties have generated in the first place.

Not only had the founding fathers been inexperienced with mass, "modern" parties, for there had as yet been no such development, but many of them *had* experienced "factions" in England, and from that experience they had come to fear any associations organized to put the interests of one group against those of another. Richard Hofstadter has reminded us that:

> American thought on this subject drew on English experience, and that most Englishmen looked back with relief upon the passing of that long, convulsive epoch of English history that occupied the seventeenth century and the first two decades of the eighteenth, in which they saw clear [factions] at work, with consequences they disliked to contemplate (1972: 11–12).

By the time of America's founding:

> Party had come to be conventionally condemned by political writers on three separate but not inconsistent grounds. First, they often postulated that society should be pervaded by concord and governed by a consensus that approached, if it did not attain, unanimity. Party, and the malicious and mendacious spirit it encouraged were believed only to create social conflicts that would not otherwise occur, or to aggravate dangerously those that normally would occur. . . . Second, a party or faction was very likely to become the instrument with which some small and narrow special interest could impose its will upon the whole of society, and hence to become the agent of tyranny. . . . Finally, the party, with its capacity to arouse malice and hostility and to command loyalty to a political entity much narrower and less legitimate than the 'public good' as a whole, was considered to be a force directly counterposed to civic virtue (Hofstadter, 1972: 12–13).

It was this type of thinking that led to George Washington's famous warning of "the baneful effects of the spirit of party generally."

And yet, if the early American environment was hostile to the idea of partisan organization, it was also in some ways uniquely suited to be the birthplace of modern political parties. As Chambers has argued, the forces *favorable* to the formation of parties included (1) the broad suffrage resulting in a large mass of voters for political leaders to deal with (preceding the extension of the suffrage in England by several decades) and (2) a new nation that already had enough national identity and unity to allow "a basic consensus on political means," including a basic liberal view that "did much to reduce the fear of parties and even of opposition parties" (1963: 1–16).

Still, parties were not a natural, *inevitable* consequence of these forces, but were instead "ingeniously shaped 'artifacts,' in the sense of structures built up over years by the industrious, if often groping, activities of men" (Chambers, 1963: 10). In fact, argues Chambers, "no man could have said in advance just what the outcome would be."

America Today: An Alternative on the Horizon?

But that outcome, however unnatural, has become an American institution. Though a degree of antiparty feelings remains a part of American political culture, it is doubtful that most Americans could conceive of a politics without parties. But as public support for the parties declines and as postindustrialism seemingly alters the field on which the parties have traditionally done battle, we must wonder whether Americans are (or will be) again "groping" for machinery better suited to organizing democratic politics in the new environment: to carry on the functions of aggregating and articulating interests, educating voters about candidates and issues, and organizing the recruitment and selection of governmental leaders.

Just as it would have been impossible to predict the development of parties two centuries ago, it may be impossible now to focus clearly on the machinery that would replace them. However, we have already considered some of the possible components. Interest groups have already shown themselves capable of articulating at least some of the many interests seeking the attention of the government. And public opinion polls inform politicians of mass opinion on selected issues. The mass media have proved themselves an efficient and relatively effective means of "educating" voters on both candidates and issues. And parties have already become largely irrelevant to the apparatus of the primary election, which has become the means today of "keeping the gate" for would-be governmental leaders.

But could such tools adequately *replace* political parties? Will their further development necessarily result in the parties' obsolescence?

Parties and Alternatives in America's Future: An Evaluation

Just as many found fault with parties before their development, so there are many today who do not welcome the thought of politics by interest groups and the media to the exclusion of political parties. No shortage of faults have been found in the growing role of interest groups, for instance. The specter of having interest groups, rather than parties, organize our politics raises these questions among others:

1. Whereas parties have aided voters by shortening the list of issues on the political agenda and limiting the range of alternatives, would not the 6000+ interest groups vying for space in the arena lead to massive confusion rather than clarity?
2. Can a long list of interest group endorsements ever replace the party label in simplifying choices among candidates for a populus that is basically undereducated and disinterested politically?
3. Though the party label today may be an inadequate cue for holding legislators accountable, would interest group politics provide a better alternative?
4. The two American parties, despite the fears of the founding fathers, have unified more than they have divided the popula-

tion; might not interest groups be more likely to accomplish the "baneful division" that Washington feared? (Put another way, interest group politics has emphasized articulation almost to the exclusion of aggregation.)

5. Where altruism has been at least one consideration in much of the history of party politics, the basic, defining characteristic of interest groups is *self-interest*.[14] Where would that leave those segments of the population without the resources to support strong interest groups?

And although party responsibility in the national government (including the link of the presidential and congressional parties) has been weak indeed, it is difficult to see how interest groups could serve to better organize the actions of government.

As for the mass media's performing the educational and agenda-setting functions, Polsby (1980: 64–65) has argued that the growing importance of the media (especially in the nominating process) has resulted in a "mass persuasion system," some negative characteristics of which are:

1. "The intensity of short-term trends of opinion are amplified. Political leaders may come to believe that certain behavior is strongly demanded of them when it in fact has only weak and transitory support in the populace."
2. Fads tend to result from "the geographic spread of sentiments (both real and imputed) from areas where they exist to areas where they do not."
3. The media tends to "interpret equivocal or incoherent events —as most are—authoritatively.... Are looters expressing legitimate social grievances, or should they be shot?"
4. "Elites do not disappear under [this] system. They are, however, less accountable to one another and more subject to the constraints of popular fashion."
5. "Such a system runs on name recognition, on celebrity, and on typecasting."

Because we join in these doubts, and others, about a politics by interest groups and mass media, we certainly do not wish to suggest that parties *should be* replaced. We have noted some changes in the environment that may make it difficult for the parties *as we have known them* to regain their place of prominence in American politics. And while we cannot claim that we hold the formula for party change that would necessarily be *sufficient* for their revitalization, we can suggest some changes that we think are *necessary* to reach that end.

The parties themselves, as well as those who believe that this country's democratic system would suffer without viable parties, should take note of the changes that have already taken place within the American environment. In the light of those changes, they should reconsider the arguments of those who have longed for more "responsible" parties, which we have argued may be more suited to the changed environs than the traditionally weak and incohesive parties of the past. Though both the Democrats and Republicans have recently undergone some changes (but of different dimensions), neither party can claim as yet to have a "strong" national organization, relative either to the parties of most other nations or to what the changed American environment would seem to allow.

In addition to strengthening themselves internally, the parties should, to the extent possible, "tune up" the statutory layer of the environment that we have suggested may be more malleable than other environmental characteristics; specific recommendations must include de-emphasizing the role of the primary election and providing a role for the party as a conduit for federal campaign funds. Finally, the parties should *take full advantage of* the new tools of campaigning, rather than allowing themselves to *be replaced* by them. The parties will regain importance to the extent that they, rather than independent forces, become the central providers of public opinion polls, computer services, and media expertise for the candidates. The Republican party has already made strides in this direction, as noted in Chapter 7; the Democrats might well follow suit.[15] The parties should use the media to promote *themselves* as well as their candidates. The Democrats brushed with this idea in the telethons that have now been placed in moth balls, and the Republicans made effective use of a national advertising campaign in 1980 that could serve as a model for such efforts in the future.[16] And even if the new politics does provide an important role for interest groups, that need not imply an insignificant role for the parties, which could still function to winnow the choices and provide moderate, consistent alternative programs. In the new politics, parties could well serve as channels for the inputs of interest groups, as well as the masses, to the government. While the parties "as we have known them" may be ineffective in the new American politics, that need not suggest that the parties are incapable of *conforming* to the changed circumstances.

As Crotty has argued, "The burden [for revitalizing the parties] would appear to be on the parties themselves to prove their relevance to a changing society and to execute with some degree of effectiveness the responsibilities to which they have fallen heir" (1977: 261). Those who have a personal stake in the continuation of party organization, or who feel strongly that the country does, might well encourage the parties to continue to "change themselves" with more direct focus on the goal of becoming truly strong national parties.

It is indeed ironic that the Republican party, the party of decentralization, which continues to espouse that principle for its own internal organization, should have developed the tools by which control could otherwise be wielded over its office holders and the more local party organs. At the same time, the Democrats, whose tools are far more meager, have displayed a tendency toward more nationalization in some of their recent, controversial, and highly publicized reforms. It is difficult to assess which party would have more difficulty in completing the "transformation"—the Republicans, whose primary constraints are ideological and hence political, or the Democrats, whose primary constraint would seem to be financial, with party infighting a major factor in its money woes.

Although there is no simple map for the parties to follow on their way to reinvigoration, the basic direction seems clear. The modest but potentially significant steps that both parties have already taken toward building more effective national parties could still prove to be just the first steps on a path leading to a new vitality for the American party system.

NOTES

1. See Angus Campbell, "A Classification of the Presidential Election," in Campbell et al. (1966), pp. 63–77. See also Flanigan and Zingale (1979), pp. 35–42; V. O. Key, "A Theory of Critical Elections," *Journal of Politics*, Vol. 17 (1955), pp. 3–18; Walter Dean Burnham (1970) pp. 32–33; and Feigert and Conway (1976), pp. 27–32.

2. See Ladd and Hadley (1978), pp. 195–6.

3. See note 7.

4. See Ronald Inglehart, *The Silent Revolution* (Princeton: Princeton University Press, 1977). See also Ladd and Hadley (1978), Chaps. 4 and 5, and Feigert and Conway (1976), p. 29.

5. In 1978 right-to-life groups claimed an impact in several congressional races but seemed most proud of the victory of anti-abortion candidate Roger Jepsen over incumbent Iowa Senator Dick Clark. In 1979 anti-abortion groups also played a part in the successful campaign of Thomas Petri to fill the vacancy created by the death of Representative William Steiger of Wisconsin.

6. See Thurow (1980) for a discussion of issues involved in "zero-sum politics."

7. According to McWilliams (in Pomper, 1981: 182–183), "Reagan preferred to run as a New Dealer grown conservative, and that stance persuaded millions of voters that he was safe enough to afford them the luxury of dumping Carter." When Democrats attempted to paint Reagan as what Pomper recalls as "a threat to the social welfare benefits of the aged, poor, and minorities," Reagan responded effectively by depicting Carter as a "great deceiver" and by playing down the conservatism that had won him the nomination (see Pomper, 1981: 78–81). And even after claiming a "conservative" mandate in the 1980 election, Reagan was quick to announce that seven "safety net" programs (Medicare, Head Start, Social Security retirement benefits, veterans' disability pro-

grams, supplemental benefits for the blind, school lunch and breakfast programs, summer youth jobs program) would not receive major cuts in the new administration's first budget (see Congressional Quarterly, *Weekly Report*, 1981: 312).

8. A few months after the election, a Harris survey (as reported in the *Houston Post* of January 27, 1981) found that "by a 3-to-2 margin, Americans oppose an outright abolition of welfare" and "by a 5-to-4 margin, a majority of Americans opposes cuts in the federal individual income tax." In her analysis of CBS/*New York Times* polls, Kathleen Frankovic (in Pomper, 1981: 113–115) also found substance to the claim that 1980 did not signal a dramatic shift to the right: "In 1980, voters were no more likely to call themselves conservatives than they were in 1976. . . . Furthermore, there is no indication that the electorate in 1980 was significantly more conservative on *specific* issues than it had been four years before. . . . Fewer voters now favored an increase in domestic spending, but more felt that domestic spending should be maintained at the same level." According to Warren Miller (as reported in *ISR Newsletter*, Spring 1981: 6), additional evidence that the 1980 elections did not signal a dramatic surge in conservatism is the fact many liberal Democrats who lost their Senate seats in 1980 had won them only narrowly in the "anti-Watergate" elections of 1974 and that conservative Senate Democrats fared as badly as liberals in the 1980 elections. Also inconsistent with the "conservative surge" theory, according to Miller, is the fact that "tax revolt" referenda were not strongly supported by the voters in several states.

9. Pomper (1981: 86) argues that "the weight of the evidence is that the 1980 election was a negative landslide based on dissatisfaction with Carter and his record rather than a direct endorsement of conservative philosophy."

10. See, for instance, Daniel Bell, *The Coming of the Post-Industrial Society*, (New York: Basic Books, 1973).

11. As reported in the *Houston Chronicle*, 22 October 1978, sec. 4, p. 5.

12. The last figure is from a study by Public Citizen's Congress Watch, as reported in "Conservative Groups Spent $13 Million on '80 Campaign," *Houston Chronicle* 22 April 1981, sec. 1, p. 7. The estimates of total PAC and party contributions were provided by the press office of the Federal Election Commission by telephone on June 30, 1981, and from an FEC press release dated August 4, 1981.

13. For an account of such claims by NCPAC and other conservative groups in the 1980 elections, see Congressional Quarterly, *Weekly Report* (1980: 3372–3373).

14. In his farewell address, President Jimmy Carter alluded to the problem of interest groups de-emphasizing the "common good": "Today, as people have become more doubtful of the ability of government to deal with our problems, we are increasingly drawn to single-issue groups and special-interest organizations to ensure that whatever else happens our own personal views and our own private interests are protected. This is a disturbing factor in American political life. It tends to distort our purposes because the national interest is not always the sum of all our single or special interests. We are all Americans together, and we must not forget that the common good is our common interest and our individual responsibility."

15. Following the 1980 elections, a number of key Democrats endorsed the idea of copying the Republicans' new election machinery (see Congressional

Quarterly, *Weekly Report*, 1981: 137–140). Upon being elected Democratic national chairman in February 1981, Charles Manatt assessed his party as "out-conceptualized, out-financed and out-worked" in 1980 and pledged to renew the party "from top to bottom" (as reported in Jerome R. Watson, "New Dem Chief Pledges 'Top to Bottom' Renewal," *Houston Chronicle*, 1 March 1981, sec. 1, p. 4).

16. As noted by the RNC's Director of Political Affairs in 1980, the national party "undertook for the first time in political history in the United States, institutional advertising of a political nature. Between five... and nine... million dollars was expended on an advertising campaign to make the general public aware that the Democrats had been in control of Congress for some twenty-five... years" (Cotten, 1981). Part of the advertising campaign stressed the theme: "Vote Republican. For a Change."

References

Aldrich, Howard, and Jeffrey Pffeffer. (1976) "Environments of Organizations." *Annual Review of Sociology*, Vol. 2, pp. 79–105. (Palo Alto: Annual Reviews.)

American Political Science Association. (1950) "Toward a More Responsible Two-Party System; a Report of the Committee on Political Parties, American Political Science Association." *American Political Science Review*, Vol. 44 (September), supplement.

Banfield, Edward. (1964) 'In Defense of the American Party System." In Robert A. Goldwin, ed., *Political Parties, U.S.A.* Chicago: Rand McNally, pp. 21–39.

Banks, Arthur. (1971) *A Cross-Polity Time Series.* Cambridge, Mass.: MIT Press.

———, and Robert Textor. (1963) *A Cross-Polity Survey.* Cambridge, Mass.: MIT Press.

Bibby, John F. (1980) "Party Renewal in the National Republican Party." In Gerald M. Pomper, ed., *Party Renewal in America: Theory and Practice.* New York: Praeger, pp. 102–115.

Blank, Robert H. (1980) *Political Parties: An Introduction.* Englewood Cliffs, N.J.: Prentice-Hall.

Blondel, Jean. (1969) *An Introduction to Comparative Government.* New York: Praeger.

———. (1973) *Comparative Legislatures.* Englewood Cliffs, N.J.: Prentice-Hall.

———. (1978) *Political Parties.* London; Wildwood House.

Brady, David W., Joseph Cooper, and Patricia Hurly. (1979) "The Decline of Party in the U.S. House of Representatives, 1887–1968." *Legislative Studies Quarterly*, Vol. 4 (August), pp. 381–407.

Braibanti, Ralph. (1968) "Comparative Political Analytics Reconsidered." *Journal of Politics*, Vol. 30 (February), pp. 25–65.

Broder, David. (1972) *The Party's Over: The Failure of Politics in America.* New York: Harper and Row.

Bryce, James. (1921) *Modern Democracies*. New York: Macmillan.

Buckholts, Paul. (1966) *Political Geography*. New York: Ronald.

Budge, Ian, et al., eds. (1976) *Party Identification and Beyond*. London: Wiley.

Burke, Edmund. (1770, 1975) "Thoughts on the Cause of the Present Discontents." In B. W. Hill, ed., *Edmund Burke on Government, Politics and Society*. Britain: Harvester.

Burnham, W. D. (1970) *Critical Elections and the Mainsprings of American Politics*. New York: Norton.

Butler, David. (1955) "American Myths about British Parties." *Virginia Quarterly Review*, Vol. 31 (Winter), pp. 46–56. Also in Garold Thumm and Edward Janosik, eds., *Parties and the Governmental System*. Englewood Cliffs, N.J.: Prentice-Hall, 1967, pp. 271–277.

Campbell, Angus, et al. (1966) *Elections and the Political Order*. New York: Wiley.

Casselini, C. W. (1961) *The Politics of Freedom: An Analysis of the Modern Democratic State*. Seattle: University of Washington Press.

Chambers, William N. (1963) *Political Parties in a New Nation*. New York: Oxford University Press.

Charlot, Monica. (1975) "The Ideological Distance between the Two Major Parties in Britain." *European Journal of Political Research*, Vol. 3, pp. 173–180.

Congressional Quarterly. (1978) *Electing Congress*. Washington, D.C.

———. (1980) *Elections '80*. Washington, D.C.

Cotten, Ben. (1981) Personal letter from the General Counsel, Republican National Committee. Dated February 6.

Cotter, Cornelius P., and John F. Bibby. (1980) "Institutional Development of Parties and the Thesis of Party Decline." *Political Science Quarterly*, Vol. 95 (Spring, pp. 1–27.

Crotty, William J. (1967) "The Party Organization and Its Activities." In William Crotty, ed., *Approaches to the Study of Party Organizations*. Boston: Allyn and Bacon, pp. 247–306.

———. (1977) *Political Reform and the American Experience*. New York: Thomas Y. Crowell.

———. (1978) *Decisions for Democrats*. Baltimore: Johns Hopkins University Press.

———, and Gary C. Jacobson. (1980) *American Parties in Decline*. Boston: Little, Brown.

Dahl, Robert A. (1967) *Pluralist Democracy in the United States*. Chicago: Rand McNally.

———. (1981) *Democracy in the United States*. Boston: Houghton Mifflin.

Dennis, Jack. (1966) "Support for the Party System by the Mass Public." *American Political Science Review*, Vol. 60 (September), pp. 600–615.

———. (1975) "Trends in Public Support for the American Party System." *British Journal of Political Science*, Vol. 5, pp. 187–230.

Dodd, Lawrence C., and Bruce Oppenheimer, eds. (1981) *Congress Reconsidered*. Washington, D.C.: Congressional Quarterly.

Duchacek, Ivo. (1970) *Comparative Federalism: The Territorial Dimension of Politics*. Chicago: Holt.

Duverger, Maurice. (1961, 1963, 1964b) *Political Parties: Their Organization and Activity in the Modern State*. London: Lowe and Brydone, 1964. Originally published in 1951. Published in 1961 and 1963 by Wiley.

———. (1964a) "Electoral Systems and Political Life." In Roy C. Macridis and Bernard E. Brown, eds., *Comparative Politics: Notes and Readings*. Homewood, Ill: Dorsey, pp. 251–264.

———. (1972) *Party Politics and Pressure Groups*. New York: Thomas Y. Crowell.

Eckstein, Harry. (1963) "The Impact of Electoral Systems on Representative Government." In Harry Eckstein and David Apter, eds., *Comparative Politics*. New York: Free Press, pp. 247–254.

———, and Ted Robert Gurr. (1975) *Patterns of Authority: Structural Basis for Political Inquiry*. New York: Wiley.

Elazar, Daniel. (1972) *American Federalism: A View from the States*. 2d Ed. New York: Thomas Y. Crowell.

Epstein, Leon D. (1967a) *Political Parties in Western Democracies*. New York: Praeger.

———. (1967b) "Political Parties in Western Democratic Systems." In Roy C. Macridis, ed., *Political Parties: Contemporary Trends and Ideas*. New York: Harper and Row, pp. 118–148.

———. (1975) "Political Parties." In Fred I. Greenstein and Nelson W. Polsby, eds., *Handbook of Political Science*, Vol. 4. Reading, Mass.: Addison-Wesley, pp. 229–277.

Evan, William M. (1976) *Organization Theory: Structure, Systems, and Environment*. New York: Wiley.

Everson, David H. (1980) *American Political Parties*. New York: New Viewpoints.

Flanigan, William, and Nancy Zingale. (1979) *Political Behavior of the American Electorate*. 4th Ed. Boston: Allyn and Bacon.

Feigert, Frank B., and Margaret M. Conway. (1976) *Parties and Politics in America*. Boston: Allyn and Bacon.

Fenno, Richard E. (1978) *Home Style: House Members in Their Districts*. Boston: Little, Brown.

Finlay, David J., et al. (1974) "The Concept of Left and Right in Cross-National Research." *Comparative Political Studies*, Vol. 7 (July), pp. 209–221.

Gelb, Joyce, and Marian Palley. (1975) *Tradition and Change in American Party Politics*. New York: Thomas Y. Crowell.

Gross, F. (1974) *The Revolutionary Party*. Westport, Conn.: Greenwood.

Gurr, Ted Robert. (1974) "Persistence and Change in Political Systems, 1800–1971." *American Political Science Review*, Vol. 68 (December), pp. 1482–1504. Data available from ICPSR, Ann Arbor.

Hall, Richard H. (1977) *Organizations: Structure and Process*. Englewood Cliffs, N.J.: Prentice-Hall.

Harmel, Robert. (1977) "Relative Impacts of Contextual and Internal Factors on Party Decentralization: A Cross-National Analysis." Ph.D. Dissertation, Northwestern University.

———. (1978) "The Relative Impacts of Country-Level and Party-Level Factors on Party Decentralization: A Cross-National Analysis." Paper delivered at the 1978 Annual Meeting of the Southwestern Political Science Association, April 12–15, Houston.

———. (1979a) "Environmental Limits on Party Ideology: A Cross-National Analysis." Paper delivered at the 1979 Annual Meeting of the Southwestern Political Science Association, March 28–31, Fort Worth.

———. (1979b) "America's Decentralized Parties in a Changing Environment: Remnants of a By-gone Era?" Paper delivered at the 1979 Annual Meeting of the Midwest Political Science Association, April 19–21, Chicago.

———. (1981) "Environment and Party Decentralization: A Cross-National Analysis." *Comparative Political Studies*, Vol. 14 (April), pp. 75–99.

Heller, Walter. (1966) *New Dimensions of Political Economy*. Cambridge: Harvard University Press.

Hermens, F. A. (1938) *Democracy or Anarchy*. Notre Dame: University of Notre Dame Press.

Hewitt, Christopher. (1977) "The Effect of Political Democracy and Social Democracy on Equality in Industrial Societies: A Cross-National Comparison." *American Sociological Review*, Vol. 42 (June), pp. 450–464.

Heydebrand, Wolf V. (1973) *Comparative Organizations: The Results of Empirical Research*. Englewood Cliffs N.J.: Prentice-Hall.

Hilton, Gordon. (1976) *Intermediate Politometrics*. New York: Columbia University Press.

Hitlin, Robert, and John Jackson. (1975) "The Democratic Party and the Responsible Parties Model." Paper presented at the 1975 Annual Meeting of the Midwest Political Science Association, Chicago.

Hofstadter, Richard, (1972) *The Idea of a Party System*. Berkeley: University of California Press.

Inglehart, Ronald. (1977) *The Silent Revolution*. Princeton: Princeton University Press.

Janda, Kenneth. (1978) "*Validating a Conceptual Framework for Comparing Political Parties..*" Evanston, Ill.: ICPP Reports, No. 18. Mimeograph.

———. (1979A) *Comparative Political Parties Data: 1950–1962*. Ann Arbor: Inter-University Consortium for Political and Social Research.

———. (1979b) "Variations in Party Organizations across Nations and Differences in Party Performance." Paper delivered at the 1979 Annual Meeting of the American Political Science Association, August 31–September 3, Washington, D.C.

———. (1980a) *Political Parties: A Cross-National Survey*. New York: Free Press.

———. (1980b) "A Comparative Analysis of Party Organizations: U.S., Europe, and the World.' In William J. Crotty, ed., *The Party Symbol*. San Francisco: Freeman, pp. 339–358.

Keefe, William. (1972, 1976, 1980) *Parties, Politics, and Public Policy in America*. New York: Holt. First edition, 1972. Third edition, 1980. Second edition, 1976, Dryden.

Key, V. O. (1964) *Politics, Parties, and Pressure Groups*. 5th Ed. New York: Thomas Y. Crowell.

Kirkpatrick, E. M. (1971) "Toward a More Responsible Two-Party System: Political Science, Policy Science, or Pseudo-Science?" *American Political Science Review*, Vol. 65 (December), pp. 965–990.

Kirkpatrick, Jeanne Jordon. (1978) *Dismantling the Parties: Reflections on Party Reform and Party Decomposition*. Washington, D.C.

Ladd, C. E., Jr. (1970) *American Political Parties: Social Changes and Political Response*. New York: Norton.

————. (1977) "Reform' Is Wrecking the U.S. Partty System." *Fortune*, November, pp. 177–188.

————. (1978) *Where Have All the Voters Gone?* New York: Norton.

————, and Charles D. Hadley. (1975, 1978) *Transformation of the American Party System*. New York: Norton. First edition, 1975. Second edition, 1978.

Lawson, Kay. (1976) *The Comparative Study of Political Parties*. New York: St. Martin's.

Legg, Keith R. (1968) *Politics in Modern Greece*. Stanford: Stanford University Press.

Lipson, Leslie. (1953) "The Two-Party System in British Politics." *American Political Science Review*, Vol. 47 (March), pp. 337–358.

Loewenberg, Gerhard, and Samuel C. Patterson. (1979) *Comparing Legislatures*. Boston: Little, Brown.

Longley, Charles. (1976) "Party Reform and Party Nationalization: The Case of the Democrats." Paper presented at the 1976 Annual Meeting of the Midwest Political Science Association, April 29–May 1, Chicago.

————. (1980a) "Party Reform and Party Nationalization: The Case of the Democrats." In William J. Crotty, ed., *The Party Symbol*. San Francisco: W. H. Freeman, pp. 359–378.

————. (1980b) "National Party Renewal." In Gerald M. Pomper, ed., *Party Renewal in America*. New York: Praeger, pp. 69–86.

McDonald, Ronald H. (1971) *Party Systems and Elections in Latin America*. Chicago: Markham.

Madron, T., and Carl Chelf. (1974) *Political Parties in the United States*. Boston: Holbrook.

Mayer, Lawrence. (1972) *Comparative Political Inquiry*. Homewood Ill.: Dorsey.

Mayo, H. B. (1960) *An Introduction to Democratic Theory*. New York: Oxford University Press.

Merkl, Peter, ed. (1980) *Western European Party Systems*. New York: Free Press.

Mezey, Michael L. (1979) *Comparative Legislatures*. Chapel Hill, N.C.: Duke University Press.

Milnor, Andrew, ed. (1969) *Comparative Political Parties*. New York: Thomas Y. Crowell.

Olson, David M. (1980) *The Legislative Process: A Comparative Approach*. New York: Harper and Row.

Ozbudun, Ergun. (1970) "Party Cohesion in Western Democracies: A Causal Analysis." Sage Professional Papers in Comparative Politics. Beverly Hills: Sage Publications.

Payne, James L. (1968) *Patterns of Conflict in Colombia*. New Haven: Yale University Press.

Pennock, J. Roland. (1979) *Democratic Political Theory*. Princeton: Princeton University Press.

Perrow, Charles. (1972) *Complex Organizations: A Critical Essay*. Glenview, Ill.: Scott Foresman.

Polsby, Nelson W. (1975) "Legislatures." In Fred I. Greenstein and Nelson W.

Polsby, eds., *Handbook of Political Science*, Vol. 5. Reading, Mass.: Addison-Wesley, pp. 257–319.

———. (1980) "The News Media as an Alternative to Party in the Presidential Selection Process." In Robert Goldwin, ed., *Political Parties in the Eighties*. Washington, D.C.: American Enterprise Institute, pp. 50–66.

Pomper, Gerald M. (1971) "Toward a More Responsible Two-Party System? What, Again?" *Journal of Politics*. Vol. 33 (November), pp. 916–940.

———, ed. (1981) *The Election of 1980*. Chatham, N.J.: Chatham House.

———, ed. (1980) *Party Renewal in America: Theory and Practice. New York:* Praeger.

Pride, Richard A. (1970) "Origins of Democracy: A Cross-National Study of Mobilization, Party Systems, and Democratic Stability." Sage Professional Papers: Comparative Politics Series. Beverly Hills: Sage Publications.

Przeworski, Adam, and Henry Teune. (1970) *The Logic of Comparative Social Inquiry*. New York: Wiley.

Ranney, Austin. (1954) *The Doctrine of Responsible Party Government*. Urbana, Ill.: University of Illinois Press.

———. (1975) *Curing the Mischiefs of Faction: Party Reform in America*. Berkeley: University of California Press.

Reagan, Michael. (1972) *The New Federalism*. New York: Oxford University Press.

Reimer, Neil. (1962) *The Revival of Democratic Theory*. New York: Appleton-Century-Crofts.

Republican National Committee. (1981) *The Chairman's Report*. Washington, D.C.

———. (1961) *The 1960 Elections: A Summary Report with Supporting Tables*. Washington, D.C.

Riker, William. (1964) *Federalism: Origin, Operation, Significance*. Boston: Little Brown.

Rokkan, Stein. (1970) *Citizens, Elections, Parties*. New York: McKay.

Robinson, Donald A. (1979) "Why Is It Hard to Strengthen Parties: Notes on the Place of Party in Democratic Ideas." Paper prepared for the Annual Meeting of the American Political Science Association, August 31–September 3, Washington, D.C.

Ross, Marc Howard, and Elizabeth Homer. (1976) "Galton's Problem in Cross-National Research." *World Politics*, Vol. 29 (October), pp. 1–28.

Rossiter, Clinton. (1960) *Parties and Politics in America*. Ithaca, N.Y.: Cornell University Press.

Rubin, Richard L. (1980) "Presidential Primaries, Continuities, Dimensions of Change, and Political Implications." In William J. Crotty, ed., *The Party Symbol*. San Francisco: W. H. Freeman, pp. 126–147.

Sartori, Giovanni. (1976) *Parties and Party Systems: A Framework for Analysis*. New York: Cambridge University Press.

Schattschneider, E. E. (1942) *Party Government*. New York: Holt.

——— (1965) "The Nationalization of Politics." In John Owens and P. J. Staudenraus, eds., *The American Party System*. New York: MacMillan, pp. 427–436.

Schlesinger, Joseph A. (1968) "Party Units." *International Encyclopedia of the Social Sciences*. New York: Macmillan, pp. 428–436.

Schumpeter, Joseph A. (1950) *Capitalism, Socialism, and Democracy.* 3d Ed. New York: Harper and Row.

Schwarz, John E., and L. Earl Shaw. (1976) *The United States Congress in Comparative Perspective.* Hinsdale, Ill.: Dryden Press.

Scott, Ruth K., and Ronald J. Hrebenar. (1979) *Parties in Crisis: Party Politics in America.* New York: Wiley.

Sigelman, Lee, and Syng Nam Yough. (1978) "Left-Right Polarization in National Party Systems: A Cross-National Analysis." *Comparative Political Studies,* Vol. 2 (October), pp. 355–379.

Smith, T. Lynn, and Paul Zopf. (1976) *Demography: Principles and Methods.* Port Washington, N.Y.: Alfred.

Sorauf, Frank J. (1972, 1980) *Party Politics in America.* 4th Ed. Boston: Little, Brown, 1980.

Stinchcombe, Arthur. (1965) "Social Structure and Organizations." In James G. March, ed., *Handbook of Organizations.* Chicago: Rand McNally, pp. 142–193.

Thomas, John. (1975) "The Decline of Ideology in Western Political Parties: A Study of Changing Policy Orientations." Sage Professional Papers in Comparative Politics. Beverly Hills: Sage Publications.

Thurow, Lester C. (1980) *The Zero-Sum Society.* New York: Basic Books.

Truman, David. (1955) "Federalism and the Party System." In Arthur Macmahon, ed., *Federalism: Mature and Emergent.* Garden City, N.Y.: Doubleday, pp. 115–136.

Turner, Julius, and Edward V. Schneier. (1970) *Party and Constituency: Pressures on Congress.* Baltimore: The Johns Hopkins Press.

Wilson, James Q. (1973) *Political Organizations.* New York: Basic Books.

APPENDIX A

Toward a More Responsible Two-Party System: Summary and Conclusions*

SUMMARY OF CONCLUSIONS AND PROPOSALS

PART I. THE NEED FOR GREATER PARTY RESPONSIBILITY

1. The Role of the Political Parties

1. *The Parties and Public Policy.* Popular goverment in a nation of more than 150 million people requires political parties which provide the electorate with a proper range of choice between alternatives of action. In order to keep the parties apart, one must consider the relations between each and public policy. The reasons for the growing emphasis on public policy in party politics are to be found, above all; in the very operations of modern government.

2. *The New Importance of Program.* The crux of public affairs lies in the necessity for more effective formulation of general policies and programs and for better integration of all of the far-flung activities of modern government. It is in terms of party programs that political leaders can attempt to consolidate public attitudes toward the work plans of government.

3. *The Potentialities of the Party System.* The potentialities of the two-party system are suggested, on the one hand, by the fact that for all practical purposes the major parties monopolize elections; and, on the other, by the fact that both parties have in the past managed to adapt themselves to the demands made upon them by external necessities. It is good practical politics to reconsider party organization in the light of the changing conditions of politics. Happily such an effort entails an application of ideas about the party system that are no longer unfamiliar.

2. What Kind of Party System Is Needed?

The party system that is needed must be democratic, responsible and effective.

* From the *American Political Science Review*, 44, II (September 1950), pp. 1–14.

I. A Stronger Two-Party System

1. *The Need for an Effective Party System.* An effective party system requires, first, that the parties are able to bring forth programs to which they commit themselves and, second, that the parties possess sufficient internal cohesion to carry out these programs. Such a degree of unity within the parties cannot be brought about without party procedures that give a large body of people an opportunity to share in the development of the party program.

2. *The Need for an Effective Opposition Party.* The fundamental requirement of accountability is a two-party system in which the opposition party acts as the critic of the party in power, developing, defining and presenting the policy alternatives which are necessary for a true choice in reaching public decisions. The opposition most conducive to responsible government is an organized party opposition.

II. Better Integrated Parties

1. *The Need for a Party System with Greater Resistance to Pressure.* There is little to suggest that the phenomenal growth of interest organizations in recent decades has come to its end. The whole development makes necessary a reinforced party system that can cope with the multiplied organized pressures. Compromise among interests is compatible with the aims of a free society only when the terms of reference reflect an openly acknowledged concept of the public interest.

2. *The Need for a Party System with Sufficient Party Loyalty.* Needed clarification of party policy will not cause the parties to differ more fundamentally or more sharply than they have in the past. Nor is it to be assumed that increasing concern with their programs will cause the parties to erect between themselves an ideological wall. Parties have the right and the duty to announce the terms to govern participation in the common enterprise. The emphasis in all consideration of party discipline must be on positive measures to create a strong and general agreement on policies. A basis for party cohesion in Congress will be established as soon as the parties interest themselves sufficiently in their congressional candidates to set up strong and active campaign organizations in the constituencies.

III. More Responsible Parties

1. *The Need for Parties Responsible to the Public.* Party responsibility means the responsibility of both parties to the general public, as enforced in elections. Party responsibility to the public, enforced in elections, implies that there be more than one party, for the public can hold a party responsible only if it has a choice. As a means of achieving responsibility, the clarification of party policy also tends to keep public debate on a more realistic level, restraining the inclination of party spokesmen to make unsubtantiated statements and charges.

2. *The Need for Parties Responsible to Their Members.* Party responsibility includes also the responsibility of party leaders to the party membership, as enforced in primaries, caucuses and conventions. The external and the internal kinds of party responsibility need not conflict. Intraparty conflict will be minimized if it is generally recognized that national, state and local party leaders

have a common responsibility to the party membership. National party leaders have a legitimate interest in the nomination of congressional candidates.

3. *The Inadequacy of the Existing Party System*

I. Beginning Transition

1. *Change and Self-Examination.* Marked changes in the structure and processes of American society have necessarily affected the party system. The prevailing climate of self-examination as well as the current tendencies toward change in the party system give point to inquiries like that represented by our report.

2. *Burden of the Past.* Formal party organization in its main features is still substantially what it was before the Civil War. Under these circumstances the main trends of American politics have tended to outflank the party system.

II. Some Basic Problems

1. *The Federal Basis.* The two parties are organized on a federal basis. The national and state party organizations are largely independent of one another, without appreciable common approach to problems of party policy and strategy. The real issue is not over the federal form of organization but over the right balance of forces within this type of organization. A corollary of the kind of federalism now expressed in the party system is an excessive measure of internal separatism.

2. *The Location of Leadership.* Party organization does not vest leadership of the party as a whole in either a single person or a committee. There is at present no central figure or organ which could claim authority to take up party problems, policies and strategy.

3. *The Ambiguity of Membership.* No understandings or rules or criteria exist with respect to membership in a party. Those who suggest that elections should deal with personalities but not with programs suggest at the same time that party membership should mean nothing at all.

III. Specific Deficiencies

1. *National Party Organs.* The National Convention, as at present constituted and operated, is an unwiedly, unrepresentative and less than responsible body. The National Committee is seldom a generally influential body and much less a working body. House and Senate campaign committees do not always have a good working relationship with the National Committee. Although interest in questions of party policy has grown, the national party organs are not so constituted nor so coordinated as to make it simple for them to pay enough attention to these questions.

2. *Party Platforms.* Alternatives between the parties are defined so badly that it is often difficult to determine what the election has decided even in broadest terms. The prevailing procedure for the writing and adoption of national party platforms is too hurried and too remote from the process by which actual decisions are made to command the respect of the whole party and the electorate. The platform should be the end product of a long search for a work-

ing agreement within the party.

3. *Intraparty Democracy.* Too little consideration has been given to ways and means of bringing about a constructive relationship between the party and its members. In making the most of popular participation, the performance of American parties is very unsatisfactory.

4. *Party Research.* A party stands as much in need of research as does business enterprise or the government itself.

4. *New Demands upon Party Leadership*

I. The Nature of Modern Public Policy

1. *Broad Range of Policy.* The expanding responsibilities of modern government have brought about so extensive an interlacing of governmental action with the country's economic and social life that the need for coordinated and coherent programs, legislative as well as administrative, has become paramount. In a democracy no general program can be adopted and carried out without wide public support.

2. *Impact on the Public.* In a predominantly industrial society, public policy tends to be widely inclusive, involving in its objectives and effects very large segments of the public or even the whole country.

3. *Governmental Program Machinery.* On the side of government, in the administrative and the legislative spheres, the twin needs for program formulation and for program machinery have long been recognized. The governmental advance toward program formulation needs now to be paralleled in the political sphere proper—above all, in the party system.

II. Rise of Nation-wide Policy Issues

1. *An Historic Trend.* The changes in the nature and scope of public policy are the result of changes in the social structure and in the economy of the United States.

2. *Past and Present Factors.* There has been in recent decades a continuing decline of sectionalism. Party organization designed to deal with the increasing volume of national issues must give wide range to the national party leadership.

3. *New Interest Groups in Politics.* The economic and social factors that have reduced the weight of sectionalism have also resulted in the development of a new type of interest groups, built upon large membership. To a much greater extent than in the past, they operate as if they were auxiliary organizations of one or the other party.

5. *The Question of Constitutional Amendment*

1. *A Cabinet System?* A responsible cabinet system makes the leaders of the majority collectively accountable for the conduct of the government.

2. *Strong Parties as a Condition.* To amend the Constitution in order to create a responsible cabinet system is not a practicable way of getting more effective parties.

3. *Adaptation within the Constitution.* The parties can do much to adapt the usages under the Constitution to their purposes.

PART II. PROPOSALS FOR PARTY RESPONSIBILITY

6. *National Party Organization*

I. Principal Party Bodies

1. *The National Convention.* We assume its continuation as the principal representative and deliberative organ of the party. The convention should meet at least biennially, with easy provision for special meetings. It should also cease to be a delegate convention of unwieldy size.

2. *The National Committee.* It is highly desirable for the National Convention to reassert its authority over the National Committee through a more active participation in the final selection of the committee membership. It is also desirable that the members of the National Committee reflect the actual strength of the party within the areas they represent.

3. *The Party Council.* We propose a Party Council of 50 members. Such a Party Council should consider and settle the larger problems of party management, within limits prescribed by the National Convention; propose a preliminary draft of the party platform to the National Convention; interpret the platform in relation to current problems; choose for the National Convention the group of party leaders outside the party organizations; consider and make recommendations to appropriate party organs in respect to congressional candidates; and make recommendations to the National Convention, the National Committee or other appropriate party organs with respect to conspicuous departures from general party decisions by state or local party organizations. In presidential years, the council would naturally become a place for the discussion of presidential candidacies, and might well perform the useful function of screening these candidacies in a preliminary way. Within this Party Council there might well be a smaller group of party advisers to serve as a party cabinet.

II. Intraparty Relationships

1. *State and Local Party Organizations.* Organizational patterns of the parties are predicated on the assumption that a party committee is necessary for each electoral area. There is a growing dissatisfaction with the results of this system on the local level, especially the multiplicity of organizations. An increasing number of state legislators are noting the breakdown or lack of party responsibility and discipline and the growth of internal separatism in state government. It is necessary for both parties to reexamine their purposes and functions in the light of the present-day environment, state and local, in which they operate.

2. *Relations between National, State and Local Organizations.* Establishment of a Party Council would do much to coordinate the different party organizations, and should be pressed with that objective in mind. Regional conferences held by both parties have clearly been fruitful. Regional party organizations should be encouraged. Local party organizations should be imbued with a stronger sense of loyalty to the entire party organization and feel their responsibility for promoting the broader policies of the party. This can be done by fostering local party meetings, regularly and frequently held, perhaps monthly. The national organization may deal with conspicuous or continued disloyalty on the part of any state organization. Consideration should be given to the develop-

ment of additional means of dealing with rebellious and disloyal state organizations.

3. *Headquarters and Staff.* Both parties are now aware of the need to maintain permanent headquarters, with staff equipped for research and publicity. A beginning has been made, but much still remains to be done. Staff development at party headquarters provides the essential mechanism to enable each party to concern itself appropriately with its continuing responsibilities.

7. Party Platforms

I. Nature of the Platform

1. *Alternative Purposes.* Should the party platform be a statement of general principles representing the permanent or long-range philosophy of the party? Or should it state the party's position on immediate issues? Actually, the platform is usually made up of both the more permanent and the more fleeting elements.

2. *Interpretation of the Platform.* As a body representing the various parts of the party structure, the Party Council should be able to give authoritative and reasonably acceptable interpretations of the platform.

3. *National-State Platform Conflicts.* What is needed is better coordination in the declaration of party principles. The Party Council would be the appropriate party agency to interpret the respective platforms and determine the right position in case of conflict. There is very little likelihood indeed for the Party Council to be inconsiderate of arguable claims of state autonomy.

4. *Binding Character.* In spite of clear implications and express pledges, there has been much difference of opinion as to the exact binding quality of a platform. All of this suggests the need for appropriate machinery, such as a Party Council, to interpret and apply the national program in respect to doubts or details. When that is done by way of authoritative and continuing statement, the party program should be considered generally binding.

II. Problems of Platform-Making

1. *Method of Formulating Party Platforms.* Occasionally the state platforms are deliberately delayed until after the national platform has been adopted, in order to have a basis for conformity. Such practice is to be encouraged, and state legislation that prevents it ought to be changed. A method of platform-making that is closely related to the congressional as well as to the presidential campaign must be developed, and with more direct participation by the party members of Congress.

2. *Improvement of Platforms and Platform-Making.* In both parties, the Platform Committee or a working part of it is now appointed some weeks in advance of the National Convention. The practice of holding public hearings on the policies to be incorporated into the platform has been fairly well established. This consultation is of importance, for it makes the parties aware of the interest in particular policies.

3. *Proposals.* Party platforms should be formulated at least every two years. National platforms should emphasize general party principles and national issues. State and local platforms should be expected to conform to the national

platform on matters of general party principle or on national policies. To achieve better machinery for platform-making, the Party Council, when set up, should prepare a tentative draft well in advance of the National Convention for the consideration of the appropriate convention committee and the convention itself. Local party meetings should be held for the discussion and consideration of platform proposals.

8. *Party Organization in Congress*

I. Introduction

1. *External Factors.* A higher degree of party responsibility in Congress cannot be provided merely by actions taken within Congress. Nevertheless, action within Congress can be of decisive significance.

2. *Continuous Evolution.* The materials for responsible party operations in Congress are already on hand. The key to progress lies in making a full-scale effort to use them.

II. Tightening Up the Congressional Party Organization

1. *The Leaders.* For more than ten years now the press has carried news about regular meetings between the President and the Big Four of Congress— the Speaker of the House, the Majority Leader of the House, the Vice-President and the Majority Leader of the Senate, when the four are of the President's party. It would be an error to attempt to supplant the relationship between the Big Four and the President by some new body. Whenever it becomes necessary for the President to meet with the leaders of both parties in Congress, it is a simple matter for the Big Four to be expanded to six or eight. In the public eye a party leader like these is a spokesman for his party as a whole. It is necessary that there be broad consultation throughout the national leadership of a party before a party leader is elected in either house.

2. *The Leadership Committees.* We submit these proposals: In both the Senate and the House, the various leadership groups should be consolidated into one truly effective and responsible leadership committee for each party. Each of these four committees should be responsible not only for submitting policy proposals to the party membership, but also for discharging certain functions with respect to the committee structure and the legislative schedule. Each of the four committees should be selected or come up for a vote of confidence no less often than every two years. Occasion must be found reasonably often for the leadership committees of each party in the two houses to meet together. Furthermore, the rival leadership committees in each house should meet together on a more regular basis. A case can also be made for the four leadership groups to meet on specific occasions.

3. *Caucuses or Conferences.* More frequent meetings of the party membership in each house should be held. A binding caucus decision on legislative policy should be used primarily to carry out the party's principles and program. When members of Congress disregard a caucus decision taken in furtherance of national party policy, they should expect disapproval. The party leadership committees should be responsible for calling more frequent caucuses or conferences and developing the agenda of points for discussion.

III. Party Responsibility for Committee Structure

1. *Selection of Committee Chairmen.* It is not playing the game fairly for party members who oppose the commitments in their party's platform to rely on seniority to carry them into committee chairmanships. Party leaders have compelling reason to prevent such a member from becoming chairman—and they are entirely free so to exert their influence. The task of party leaders, when confronted with revolt on the part of committee chairmen, is not easy. Obviously problems of this sort must be handled in the electoral process itself as well as in the congressional arena.

2. *Assignment of Members Committees.* The slates of committee assignments should be drawn up by the party leadership committees and presented to the appropriate party caucuses for approval or modification. There is nothing sound in having the party ratio on the committees always correspond closely to the party ratio in the House itself. Committee assignments should be subjected to regular reexamination by the party caucus or conference with reasonable frequency.

3. *Committee Staff.* Staff assistance should be available to minority as well as majority members of a committee whenever they want it. Where all committee staff is controlled by the majority, a change in power threatens continuity of service.

IV. Party Responsibility for the Legislative Schedule

1. *The Need for Scheduling.* Schedules should be openly explained on the floor in advance. No committee should be in charge of legislative scheduling except the party leadership committee.

2. *House Guidance of Legislative Traffic.* A democratic approach would be to substitute open party control for control by the Rules Committee or individual chairmen.

3. *The Right to Vote in the Senate.* The present cloture rule should be amended. The best rule is one that provides for majority cloture on all matters before the Senate.

9. *Political Participation*

Widespread political participation fosters responsibility as well as democratic control in the conduct of party affairs and the pursuit of party policies. A more responsible party system is intimately linked with the general level as well as the forms of political participation.

I. Intraparty Democracy

1. *Party Membership.* As stress is placed by the parties upon policy and the interrelationship of problems at various levels of government, association with a party should become more interesting and attractive to many who hold aloof today.

2. *Machinery of Intraparty Democracy.* If the National Convention is to serve as the grand assembly of the party, in which diverse viewpoints are compounded into a course of action, it must be nourished from below. To this end local party groups are needed that meet frequently to discuss and initiate policy.

3. *Toward a New Concept of Party Membership.* The existence of a national program, drafted at frequent intervals by a party convention both broadly representative and enjoying prestige, should make a great difference. It would prompt those who identify themselves as Republicans or Democrats to think in terms of support of that program, rather than in terms of personalities, patronage and local matters. Once machinery is established which gives the party member and his representative a share in framing the party's objectives, once there are safeguards against internal dictation by a few in positions of influence, members and representatives will feel readier to assume an obligation to support the program. Membership defined in these terms does not ask for mindless discipline enforced from above. It generates self-discipline which stems from free identification with aims one helps to define.

II. Nominating Procedure.

1. *United States Senator and Representative.* Nominations for United States Senator and Representative are governed largely by state laws that vary radically in their provisions. National regulation would overcome the disadvantages of so much variety. But one must face the practical objections to national regulation. The direct primary probably can be adapted to the needs of parties unified in terms of national policy. The closed primary deserves preference because it is more readily compatible with the development of a responsible party system. The open primary tends to destroy the concept of membership as the basis of party organization. Cross filing is bound to obscure program differences between the parties, and to eliminate any sense of real membership on the part of the rank and file. The Washington blanket primary corrupts the meaning of party even further by permitting voters at the same primary to roam at will among the parties. The formal or informal proposal of candidates by preprimary meetings of responsible party committees or party councils is a healthy development. Quite appropriately the Party Council might become a testing ground for candidates for United States Senator or Representative.

2. *Presidential Nomination.* In the National Convention, delegates representative of the party membership should be chosen by direct vote of the rank and file. The Party Council naturally would concern itself with platform plans and the relative claims of those who might be considered for presidential and vice presidental nominations. In time it may be feasible and desirable to substitute a direct, national presidential primary for the indirect procedure of the convention.

III. Elections

1. *Election of the President.* The present method of electing the President and Vice President fosters the blight of one-party monopoly and results in concentration of campaign artillery in pivotal industrial states where minority groups hold the balance of power. In the persistent agitation for change in the Electoral College system, stress should be placed both upon giving all sections of the country a real voice in electing the President and the Vice President and upon developing a two-party system in present one-party areas.

2. *Term of Representative.* It appears desirable to lengthen the term of Representatives to four years.

3. *Campaign Funds.* Existing statutory limitations work toward a scattering of responsibility for the collecting of funds among a large number of independent party and nonparty committees. Repeal of these restrictions would make it possible for a national body to assume more responsibility in the field of party finance. The situation might be improved in still another way by giving a specified measure of government assistance to the parties. Everything that makes the party system more meaningful to all voters leads incidentally to a broadening of the base of financial support of the parties.

4. *Apportionment and Redistricting.* It is time to insist upon congressional districts approximately equal in population.

IV. Barriers to Voting

1. *Registration.* The system of permanent registration should be extended. Properly qualified newcomers to an area should be permitted to register and vote without undue delay.

2. *Access to the Polls.* Legislation establishing National Election Day would in all probability bring to the polls large numbers of people who would otherwise never come. Holding elections on Saturdays or Sundays would probably also help to increase the size of the vote. Adequate voting time should be provided by opening the booths in the earlier morning hours and keeping them open into the late evening hours. There is room for much elaboration in laws governing absentee balloting.

3. *Undemocratic Limitations.* Intentionally limiting devices should be overcome by a combination of legal change and educational efforts. Action is indicated to extend the suffrage to the inhabitants of the District of Columbia.

4. *The Short Ballot.* Adoption of the short ballot would concentrate choice on contests with program implications and thus shift attention toward issues rather than personalities.

10. *Research on Political Parties*

I. Basic Facts and Figures

1. *Election Statistics.* We propose the publication of an election yearbook by the Bureau of the Census. The arrangement of the yearbook should probably be by states. In addition, a summary booklet for presidential and congressional elections should be issued.

2. *Party Activities.* Compilation and regular publication of information on party activities are no less urgently needed.

3. *Compilation of Party Regulations.* A third task is the collection of all major regulations relating to national parties and elections.

II. More Research by the Parties

1. *Party Research Staffs.* What is needed is a stronger full-time research organization adequately financed and working on a year-in, year-out basis.

2. *Areas of Work.* There are two fields of research that should always be of immediate interest to the national organization of every party. The first is the analysis of voting trends and voting behavior. A second research field is analysis of proposals dealing with changes in election methods.

III. More Studies of the Parties

1. *Types of Research Needed.* In a field in which much still remains to be done, specific priorities have little meaning. The basic need is for a combination of creative hypotheses and realistic investigations.

2. *Professors and Politics.* The character of political research cannot be dissociated from the general approach of academic institutions to politics as a whole. Increased faculty participation in political affairs would mean more practical, realistic and useful teaching as well as research in the field of political parties.

3. *Role of Research Foundations.* The private foundations should actively solicit new ideas and proposals for research on political parties.

4. *Role of American Political Science Association.* The presentation of this report is but one instance of the interest shown in the subject of political parties by the American Political Science Association. In making specific suggestions in this field, the Association could exert a further welcome influence.

PART III. THE PROSPECT FOR ACTION

11. *Sources of Support and Leadership*

Readjustments in the structure and operation of the political parties call for a widespread appreciation, by influential parts of the public as well as by political leaders and party officials, of the kinds of change that are needed in order to bring about a more responsible operation of of the two-party system.

1. *The Economic Pressure Groups.* Highly organized special interests with small or no direct voting power are best satisfied if the individual legislator and administrative official are kept defenseless in the face of their special pressure. Organizations with large membership are not in the same category. It is reasonable to expect that those large-membership organizations with wise leadership will generally support the turn toward more responsible parties.

2. *The Party Leaders.* Leaders who represent divergent sectional or other special interests within each party will look with disfavor upon any reforms that hit specifically at their personal vested interests. Most of the forward-looking leaders in each party are convinced that changes should be made.

3. *The Government Officialdom.* Greater program responsibility at the level of the political parties is likely to appeal to administrators and the career officialdom.

4. *Congress.* It cannot be expected that all congressional leaders will be sympathetic to the concept of party responsibility. As leaders of national opinion, influential members of each party in Congress can give strong support to the idea of party responsibility.

5. *The President.* The President can probably be more influential than any other single individual in attaining a better organized majority party, and thus also prompting the minority party to follow suit. With greater party responsibility, the President's position as party leader would correspond in strength to the greater strength of his party.

6. *The Electorate.* The electorate consists of three main groups: (1) those who seldom or never vote; (2) those who vote regularly for the party of their traditional affiliation; and (3) those who base their electoral choice upon the political performance of the two parties, as indicated by the programs they support and the candidates they succeed in putting forward. The rank and file in each party want their party so organized that the views of the party majority will be respected and carried out. It may well be the members of the third group who, in making their choices at election time, will decide the question of our country's progress in the direction of a more responsible party system. It is this group that occupies a place of critical importance in supporting a party system able to shoulder national responsibility.

12. *The Dangers of Inaction*

Four dangers warrant special emphasis. The first danger is that the inadequacy of the party system in sustaining well-considered programs and providing broad public support for them may lead to grave consequences in an explosive era. The second danger is that the American people may go too far for the safety of constitutional government in compensating for this inadequacy by shifting excessive responsibility to the President. The third danger is that with growing public cynicism and continuing proof of the ineffectiveness of the party system the nation may eventually witness the disintegration of the two major parties. The fourth danger is that the incapacity of the two parties for consistent action based on meaningful programs may rally support for extremist parties poles apart, each fanatically bent on imposing on the country its particular panacea.

1. *The Danger of an Explosive Era.* The political foundation of appropriate governmental programs is very unstable when it is not supplied by responsible party action.

2. *The Danger of Overextending the Presidency.* Dependable political support has to be built up for the governmental program. When there is no other place to get that done, when the political parties fail to do it, it is tempting to turn to the President. When the President's program actually is the sole program, either his party becomes a flock of sheep or the party falls apart, This concept of the presidency disposes of the party system by making the President reach directly for the support of a majority of the voters.

3. *The Danger of Disintegration of the Two Parties.* A chance that the electorate will turn its back upon the two parties is by no means academic. As a matter of fact, this development has already occurred in considerable part, and it is still going on. American political institutions are too firmly grounded upon the two-party system to make its collapse a small matter.

4. *The Danger of an Unbridgeable Political Cleavage.* If the two parties do not develop alternative programs that can be executed, the voter's frustration and the mounting ambiguities of national policy might set in motion more extreme tendencies to the political left and the political right. Once a deep political cleavage develops between opposing groups, each group naturally works to keep it deep. Orientation of the American two-party system along the lines of meaningful national programs is a significant step toward avoiding the development of such a cleavage.

APPENDIX B

Charter of the Democratic Party of the United States

PREAMBLE

We, the Democrats of the United States of America, united in common purpose, hereby rededicate ourselves to the principles which have historically sustained our Party. Recognizing that the vitality of the Nation's political institutions has been the foundation of its enduring strength, we acknowledge that a political party which wishes to lead must listen to those it would lead, a party which asks for the people's trust must prove that it trusts the people and a party which hopes to call forth the best the Nation can achieve must embody the best of the Nation's heritage and traditions.

What we seek for our Nation, we hope for all people: individual freedom in the framework of a just society, political freedom in the framework of meaningful participation by all citizens. Bound by the United States Constitution, aware that a party must be responsive to be worthy of responsibility, we pledge ourselves to open, honest endeavor and to the conduct of public affairs in a manner worthy of a society of free people.

Under God, and for these ends and upon these principles, we do establish and adopt this Charter of thhe Democratic Party of the United States of America.

ARTICLE ONE

The Democratic Party of the United States of America

The Democratic Party of the United States of America shall:

1. Nominate and assist in the election of Democratic candidates for the offices of President and Vice President of the United States;

2. Adopt and promote statements of policy;

3. Assist state and local Democratic Party organizations in the election of their candidates and the education of their voters;

4. Establish standards and rules of procedure to afford all members of the Democratic Party full, timely and equal opportunities to participate in decisions

concerning the selection of candidates, the formulation of policy, and the conduct of other Party affairs, without prejudice on the basis of sex, race, age (if of voting age), religion, economic status or ethnic origin, and, further, to promote fair campaign practices and the fair adjudication of disputes;

5. Raise and disburse monies needed for the successful operation of the Democratic Party;

6. Work with Democratic public officials at all levels to achieve the objectives of the Democratic Party; and

7. Encourage and support codes of political ethics that embody substantive rules of ethical guidance for public officials and employees in federal, state and local governments, to assure that public officials shall at all times conduct themselves in a manner that reflects creditably upon the office they serve, shall not use their office to gain special privileges and benefits and shall refrain from acting in their official capacities when their independence of judgment would be adversely affected by personal interests or duties.

ARTICLE TWO

National Convention

Section 1. The Democratic Party shall assemble in National Convention in each year in which an election for office of President of the United States is held.

Section 2. The National Convention shall be the highest authority of the Democratic Party, subject to the provisions of this Charter. The National Convention shall recognize the state and other Parties entitled to participate in the conduct of the national affairs of the Democratic Party, including its conventions, conferences and committees. State Party rules or state laws relating to the election of delegates to the National Convention shall be observed unless in conflict with this Charter and other provisions adopted pursuant to authority of the Charter, including the resolutions or other actions of the National Convention. In the event of such conflict with state laws, state Parties shall be required to take provable positive steps to bring such laws into conformity and to carry out such other measures as may be required by the National Convention or the Democratic National Committee.

Section 3. The National Convention shall nominate a candidate for the office of President of the United States, nominate a candidate for the office of Vice President of the United States, adopt a platform and act upon such other matters as it deems appropriate.

Section 4. The National Convention shall be composed of delegates who are chosen through processes which (i) assure all Democratic voters full, timely and equal opportunity to participate and include affirmative action programs toward that end, (ii) assure that delegations fairly reflect the division of preferences expressed by those who participate in the Presidential nominating process, (iii) exclude the use of the unit rule at any level, (iv) do not deny participation for failure to pay a cost, fee or poll tax, (v) restrict participation to Democrats only, and (vi) begin within the calendar year of the Convention provided, however, that fairly apportioned and openly selected state Party Committees, elected no earlier than January 1st of the preceding mid-term Congressional election year, from states not having state conventions authorized to elect delegates shall not be precluded from selecting not more than 25% of their respective state delegations according to the standards provided in this Charter and the By-Laws.

Section 5. The delegate vote allocable to each state shall be determined as provided in the By-laws, consistent with a formula giving equal weight to population, which may be measured by electoral vote, and to the Democratic vote in elections for the office of President. The apportionment of delegates who are to be elected from units no larger than a Congressional district shall be determined by the state Democratic Party in accordance with the Call to the National Convention.

ARTICLE THREE

Democratic National Committee

Section 1. The Democratic National Committee shall have general responsibility for the affairs of the Democratic Party between National Conventions, subject to the provisions of this Charter and to the resolutions or other actions of the National Convention. This responsibility shall include: (i) issuing the call to the National Convention; (ii) conducting the Party's Presidential campaign; (iii) filling vacancies in the nominations for the office of President and Vice President; (iv) formulating and disseminating statements of Party policy; (v) providing for the election or appointment of a Chairperson, an Executive Vice Chairperson of the opposite sex, a Second Executive Vice Chairperson, a Third Executive Vice Chairperson of the opposite sex, a Treasurer, a Secretary and other appropriate officers of the National Committee and for the filling of vacancies; and (vi) all other actions necessary or appropriate in order to carry out the provisions of this Charter and the objectives of the Democratic Party.

Section 2. The Democratic National Committee shall be composed of: (i) The Chairperson and the highest ranking officer of the opposite sex of each recognized state Democratic Party; (ii) two hundred additional members apportioned to the states on the same basis as delegates to the National Convention are apportioned; provided that each state shall have at least two such additional members; (iii) the Chairperson of the Democratic Governors' Conference and two additional governors selected by the Conference (iv) the Democratic Leader in the United States Senate and the Democratic Leader in the United States House of Representatives and one additional member of each body appointed by the respective leaders; (v) the Chairperson, three Executive Vice Chairpersons, the Chairperson of the National Finance Council, the Treasurer and the Secretary of the Democratic National Committee; (vi) the Chairperson of the Conference of Democratic Mayors and two additional mayors selected by the Conference; (vii) the President of the Young Democrats of America and two additional members selected by the organization biennially in convention assembled; (viii) the Chairperson of the Democratic County Officials Conference and two additional county officials selected by the Conference; (ix) the Chairperson of the State Legislative Leaders Caucus and two additional state legislators selected by the Association; (x) the President of the National Federation of Democratic Women; and (xi) additional members as provided in Article Eleven of this Charter. No more than twenty-five additional members of the Democratic National Committee may be added by the foregoing members.

Section 3. Members of the Democratic National Committee apportioned to the states and those provided for in Article II who are not otherwise members by virtue of Party office, shall be selected by each state Democratic Party in accordance with standards as to participation established in the By-Laws of the Democratic Party for terms commencing on the day the National Convention adjourns and terminating on the day the next Convention adjourns. Such members shall be selected during the calendar year in which a National Convention is held, through processes which assure full, timely and equal opportunity to participate. Vacancies shall be filled by the state party as provided in the By-Laws. The members of the National Committee from each state shall be divided as equally as practicable between committeemen and committeewomen. Members of the Democratic National Committee who serve by virtue of holding public or party office shall serve on the Committee only during their terms in such office. Members of the Democratic National Committee added by the other members shall serve for the period designated at the time of their selection, but in no event beyond the day the next Convention adjourns. Members of the Democratic National Committee who serve by virtue of holding state Party office shall be selected by such parties in accordance with standards as to participation established in the By-Laws.

Section 4. The By-Laws may provide for removal of members of the Democratic National Committee for cause by a two-thirds vote of the National Committee and may also require continued residence in the jurisdiction represented by the member and affirmative support for the Democratic Presidential and Vice Presidential nominees as a condition of continued membership thereon.

Section 5. The Democratic National Committee shall meet at least once each year. Meetings shall be called by the Chairperson, by the Executive Committee of the Democratic National Committee, or by written request of no fewer than one-fourth of the members of the Democratic National Committee.

Section 6. The Democratic National Committee shall submit to each National Convention, prior to the commencement thereof, a written report of the activities and affairs of the Democratic Party since the preceding National Convention.

ARTICLE FOUR

Executive Committee

Section 1. There shall be an Executive Committee of the Democratic National Committee, which shall be responsible for the conduct of the affairs of the Democratic Party subject to this Charter, the National Convention and the Democratic National Committee.

Section 2. The Executive Committee shall be elected by and serve at the pleasure of the members of the Democratic National Committee. The size, composition and term of office shall be determined by the Democratic National Committee, provided that, as nearly as practicable, no fewer than one-half of the members shall be elected from regional caucuses of members of the Democratic National Committee.

Section 3. The Executive Committee shall meet at least four times each year. Meetings shall be called by the Chairperson or by written request of no fewer than one-fourth of its members. The Executive Committee shall keep a record of its proceedings which shall be available to the public.

ARTICLE FIVE

National Chairperson

Section 1. The National Chairperson of the Democratic Party shall carry out the programs and policies of the National Convention and the Democratic National Committee.

Section 2. The National Chairperson shall be elected (i) at the first meeting of the Democratic National Committee held after the National Convention, and (ii) at a meeting of the Democratic National Committee held after the succeeding presidential election and prior to March 1 next, and (iii) whenever a vacancy occurs. The National Chairperson shall be elected and may be removed by a majority vote of the Democratic National Committee, and each term shall expire upon the election for the following term.

Section 3. The National Chairperson shall preside over meetings of the Democratic National Committee and of the Executive Committee. In the absence of the National Chairperson, the next highest ranking officer of the National Committee present at the meeting shall preside.

Section 4. The National Chairperson shall serve full time and shall receive such compensation as may be determined by agreement between the Chairperson and the Democratic National Committee.

ARTICLE SIX

Party Conference

The Democratic Party may hold a National Party Conference between National Conventions. The nature, agenda, composition, time and place of the Party Conference shall be determined by the Democratic National Committee. At a meeting held during the first calendar year after each Presidential election, the Democratic National Committee shall vote upon the question of whether such Party Conference shall be held.

ARTICLE SEVEN

Judicial Council

Section 1. There shall be a Judicial Council of the Democratic Party appointed by the Democratic National Committee, the function of which shall be to adjudicate disputes arising out of the interpretation or application of national Party law, provided however, that the right of the Democratic National Convention and Democratic National Committee to settle credential disputes concerning their respective bodies shall not be abridged.

Section 2. The Democratic National Committee shall determine and provide necessary support for the Judicial Council.

ARTICLE EIGHT

National Finance Council

Section 1. The Democratic National Committee shall establish a National Finance Council, which shall have general responsibility for the finances of the Democratic Party. The National Finance Council shall raise funds to support the Democratic Party and shall advise and assist state Democratic Parties and candidates in securing funds for their purposes.

Section 2. Members of the Finance Council shall be selected and approved as provided in the By-Laws, and the Chairman of the Finance Council shall be elected or approved by the Democratic National Committee.

ARTICLE NINE

National Education and Training Council

Section 1. There shall be a National Education and Training Council of the Democratic Party, which shall be responsible for the creation and implementation of education and training programs for the Democratic Party in furtherance of its objectives. The allocation of funds to the National Education and Training Council shall be provided by the Democratic National Committee and shall be budgeted at least one year in advance of anticipated expenditures. In order to encourage a lifetime of meaningful political participation for every Democrat, the National Education and Training Council shall attempt to reach every young citizen as they enter the electorate at eighteen years of age.

Section 2. The National Education and Training Council shall be composed of (i) eight members elected by the Executive Committee and (ii) the National Chairperson.

Section 3. The National Education and Training Council shall operate under the guidance of the Executive Committee.

ARTICLE TEN

Full Participation

Section 1. The Democratic Party of the United States shall be open to all who desire to support the Party and who wish to be known as Democrats.

Section 2. Discrimination in the conduct of Democratic Party affairs on the basis of sex, race, age (if of voting age), religion, economic status or ethnic origin is prohibited, to the end that the Democratic Party at all levels be an open party.

Section 3. In order to encourage full participation by all Democrats, with particular concern for minority groups, native Americans, women and youth, in the delegate selection process and in all Party affairs, as defined in the By-Laws, the national and state Democratic Parties shall adopt and implement affirmative action programs with specific goals and time tables for achieving results.

Section 4. The goal of such affirmative action shall be to encourage representation in delegate selection processes and in Party organizations at all levels, as defined in the By-Laws, of the aforementioned groups as indicated by their presence in the Democratic electorate.

Section 5. This goal shall not be accomplished either directly or indirectly by the national or state Democratic Parties' imposition of mandatory quotas at any level of the delegate selection process or in any other Party affairs, as defined in the By-Laws.

Section 6. Performance under an approved affirmative action program and composition of the Convention delegation shall be considered relevant evidence in the challenge of any state delegation. If a state Party has adopted and implemented an approved and monitored affirmative action program, the Party shall not be subject to challenge based solely on delegate composition or solely on primary results.

Section 7. Notwithstanding Section 5 above, equal division at any level of delegate or committee positions between delegate men and delegate women or committeemen and committeewomen shall not constitute a violation of any provision thereof.

ARTICLE ELEVEN

General Provisions

Section 1. Democratic Party means the Democratic Party of the United States of America.

Section 2. The By-Laws shall provide for states in which the Democratic nominee for President or electors committed to the nominee did not appear on the ballot in elections used for apportionment formulae.

Section 3. For the purposes of this Charter, the District of Columbia shall be treated as a state containing the appropriate number of Congressional Districts.

Section 4. For the purposes of this Charter, Puerto Rico shall be treated as a state containing the appropriate number of Congressional Districts.

Section 5. Recognized Democratic Party organizations in areas not entitled to vote in Presidential elections may elect such voting delegates to National Conventions as the Democratic National Committee provides in the Call to the Convention.

Section 6. Latin American Guam, the Virgin Islands and Democrats Abroad shall each have one vote on the Democratic National Committee, which vote shall be shared by the Chairperson, highest ranking officer of the opposite sex, the National Committeeman and the National Committeewoman, except as may otherwise be provided by the By-Laws.

Section 7. The By-Laws shall provide for regional organizations of the Party.

Section 8. To assure that the Democratic nominee for the office of President of the United States is selected by a fair and equitable process, the Democratic National Committee may adopt such statements of policy as it deems appropriate with respect to the timing of Presidential primaries and shall work with state Parties to accomplish the objectives of such statements, provided, however, that such statements of policy shall not be deemed to be binding upon any states in which the state laws are in conflict with such statements.

Section 9. The Democratic National Committee shall adopt and publish a code of fair campaign practices, which shall be recommended for observance by all candidates campaigning as Democrats.

Section 10. The Democratic Party shall not require a delegate to a Party convention or caucus to cast a vote contrary to his or her expressed preference.

Section 11. Voting by proxy shall not be permitted at the National Convention. Voting by proxy shall otherwise be permitted in Democratic Party affairs only as provided in the By-Laws of the Democratic Party.

Section 12. All meetings of the Democratic National Committee, the Executive Committee, and all other official Party committees, commissions and bodies shall be open to the public, and votes shall not be taken by secret ballot.

Section 13. The Democratic National Committee shall prepare and make available to the public an annual report concerning the financial affairs of the Democratic Party.

Section 14. In the absence of other provisions, Robert's Rules of Order (as most recently revised) shall govern the conduct of all Democratic Party meetings.

Section 15. There shall be authentic texts of this Charter published in all of the official languages of these United States, which include French and Spanish, as well as English. Authentic French and Spanish texts shall be approved by the Democratic National Committee during calendar year 1975.

ARTICLE TWELVE

Amendments, By-Laws, and Rules

Section 1. This Charter may be amended by a vote of a majority of all of the delegates to the National Convention. This Charter may also be amended by a vote of two-thirds of the entire membership of the Democratic National Committee provided that at least thirty days written notice of the meeting and any proposed amendment has been given to all members of the National Committee and has been released to the national news media. This Charter may also be amended by a vote of two-thirds of the entire membership of any Democratic Party Conference called under the authority of this Charter for such purpose.

Section 2. By-Laws of the Democratic Party shall be adopted to provide for the governance of the affairs of the Democratic Party in matters not provided for in this Charter. By-Laws may be adopted or amended by a majority vote of (i) the National Convention or (ii) the Democratic National Committee provided that thirty days written notice of any proposed By-Law or amendment has been given to all members of the National Committee. Unless adopted in the form of an amendment to this Charter or otherwise designated, any resolution adopted by the National Convention relating to the governance of the Party shall be considered a By-Law.

Section 3. Each official body of the Democratic Party created under the authority of this Charter shall adopt and conduct its affairs in accordance with written rules, which rules shall be consistent with this Charter, the By-Laws and other provisions adopted pursuant to authority of the Charter, including resolutions or other actions of the National Convention. The Democratic National Committee shall maintain copies of all such rules and shall make them available upon request.

Section 4. Each recognized state Democratic Party shall adopt and conduct its affairs in accordance with written rules. Copies of such rules and of any changes or amendments thereto shall be filed with the Democratic National Committee within thirty days following adoption.

RESOLUTION OF ADOPTION

Section 1. The Democratic Party of the United States of America, assembled in a Conference on Democratic Party Organization and Policy pursuant to resolution adopted by the 1972 Democratic National Convention and the Call to the Conference hereby adopts for the governance of the Party the Charter attached hereto.

Amended as of February 27, 1981

APPENDIX C

Rules of the Republican National Party (Edited Version)

Rules Action Taken
Committee on Rules and Order of Business
REPUBLICAN NATIONAL CONVENTION
July 12–14, 1980

BE IT RESOLVED, That the Republican Party is the party of the open door. Ours is the party of equality of opportunity for all and favoritism for none.

It is the intent and purpose of these rules to encourage the broadest possible participation of all voters in the Republican Party activities at all levels and to assure that the Republican Party is open, accessible to all and answerable ultimately to the people in the true American tradition.

It is the further purpose of these rules to make certain that the Republican Party stands for the principle that while we are the party open to all, we are also the party of opportunity for all; opportunity for everyone of every race, religion, color, national origin, age or sex.

These rules provides for full participation with equal opportunity for men and women, for minorities and heritage groups, and for all Americans regardless or age of social or economic status.

These rules mandate that the Republican Party shall be a nationwide party, purposeful and strong in all sections of the country, North, South, East and West; and

BE IT FURTHER RESOLVED, That the following be adopted as the rules of business of this convention, the rules for the election and government of the Republican National Committee, the rules under which delegates and alternate delegates shall be allotted to the respective states in the next convention, and how their election shall be conducted and contests shall be considered.

Proceedings of the Convention

RULES No. 1 through 18

Republican National Committee

RULE No. 19

(a) The Republican National Committee shall have the general management of the Republican party in the United States, the District of Columbia, Guam, Puerto Rico, and the Virgin Islands, subject to direction from the national convention. The members of the national committee shall be elected by the various states and shall consist of one man and one woman from each state.

(b) The duly elected and acting chairman of each state shall be a member of the national committee during his or her tenure in office.

(c) Auxiliaries of the Republican National Committee may be recognized only by the Republican National Convention.

RULE No. 20

At each Republican National Convention called for the purpose of nominating candidates for President and Vice President, the roll shall be called and the delegation from each state shall report through its chairman the names of the elected national committee members whose election shall be ratified by the convention.

RULE No. 21

State laws providing a method of election for national committeemen and committeewomen shall be binding on the Republican National Convention.

RULE No. 22

Where state laws do not provide a method for the election of national committeemen and committeewomen, a national convention delegation shall be bound by the state party rules. The national convention may enforce these rules if they are not obeyed by the state's national convention delegation. This rule shall not apply to Republican state chairmen.

RULE No. 23

Duly elected national committeemen and national committeewomen shall serve from the adjournment of the quadrennial national convention until the adjournment of the following quadrennial national convention.

RULE No. 24

(a) The national committee shall issue the call for the next national convention to nominate candidates for President and Vice President of the United States prior to January 1 of the year in which the convention is to be held. The national committee shall issue and promulgate the call in a manner consistent with these rules.

(b) There shall be the following committees:

(1) There shall be a standing Committee on Rules of the Republican National Committee composed of one representative from each state to review and propose recommendations on changes. The representatives serving on the Republican National Committee from the several states shall choose from their number within six months following the national convention appointees to serve on this Committee. If the representatives serving on the Republican National Committee from one or more states do not within this period submit to the Chairman of the Republican National Committee their choice to serve on the

Rules Committee, the Chairman of the Republican National Committee shall select, from among the representatives serving on the Republican National Committee from such state or states, one member to serve on the Rules Committee. The Chairman of this Committee shall be elected by the Committee on Rules.

(2) There shall be a Committee on Arrangements. The chairman of the Republican National Committee shall appoint from among the members of the Republican National Committee at least one representative to the Arrangements Committee from each state. The chairman of this committee and its subcommittees shall be elected by the Committee on Arrangements, and shall be members of the executive committee of the Committee on Arrangements together with such other officers elected by the Committee on Arrangements. The chairman of the Rules Committee and the chairman of the Contest Committee shall also be members of the Arrangements Committee.

(3) There shall be a Committee on Call whose chairman and members shall be appointed by the national chairman and composed of at least seven (7) members of the Republican National Committee. This Committee to be appointed after the selection of the Committee on Arrangements and Committee on Rules.

(4) There shall be a Committee on Contests which shall be composed of two (2) members from each region elected by the members of the national committee residing in each region, and a chairman appointed by the Chairman of the national committee. This Committee shall be elected after the selection of the Rules and Arrangements Committees.

(5) There shall be a Committee on the Site of the National Convention, which shall be composed of two (2) members elected by the members of the National Committee residing in each region from their number, and a chairman appointed by the Chairman of the National Committee, which Committee shall be selected no later than two (2) years following the presidential election.

(6) Each member of the Republican National Committee shall be a member of at least one of these committees. The general counsel of the Republican National Committee shall be counsel to the above-mentioned committees. The minutes of these committees shall be distributed immediately to all members of the national committee. Any of these committees may meet and act by telephone conference upon twenty-four (24) hours notice.

RULE No. 25

(a) The officers of the national committee shall consist of:

(1) A chairman and a co-chairman of the opposite sex who shall be elected by the members of the Republican National Committee and who shall be full-time, paid employees. The chairman shall be the chief executive officer of the Republican National Committee. The chairman and co-chairman may be removed from office only by a two-thirds (2/3rds) vote of the entire national committee.

(2) Eight (8) vice chairmen, one man and one woman, from each of the following regions:

The Western States Association: Alaska, Arizona, California, Colorado, Guam, Hawaii, Idaho, Montana, Nevada, New Mexico, Oregon, Utah, Washington and Wyoming;

The Midwestern States Association: Illinois, Indiana, Iowa, Kansas, Michigan, Minnesota, Missouri, Nebraska, North Dakota, Ohio, South Dakota, West Virginia and Wisconsin;

The Northeastern States Association: Connecticut, Delaware, the District of Columbia, Maine, Maryland, Massachusetts, New Hampshire, New Jersey, New York, Pennsylvania, Puerto Rico, Rhode Island, Vermont, and the Virgin Islands;

The Southern States Association: Alabama, Arkansas, Florida, Georgia, Kentucky, Louisiana, Mississippi, North Carolina, Oklahoma, South Carolina, Tennessee, Texas and Virginia.

(3) a secretary, a treasurer, and such other officers as the committees shall deem necessary, all to be elected by the national committee.

(b) The chairman, co-chairman and all other officers except the vice chairmen shall be elected immediately following the National Convention in 1980, and in January of each odd numbered year thereafter. All officers except the vice chairmen shall be nominated from the floor, and candidates must have at least two (2) votes in three (3) states in order to have their names put in nomination. There shall be no nominating committee.

(c) The eight (8) vice chairmen shall be elected at regional caucuses by the national committee members of the four (4) regions and shall be residents and national committee members from their respective regions. The election shall take place at the first meeting after the quadrennial national convention. The election of vice chairmen does not need confirmation by the Republican National Committee.

(d) The chairman shall appoint a general counsel for the committee and a chairman of the Republican Finance Committee, both of whom shall be confirmed by the Republican National Committee at its next meeting.

RULE No. 26

(a) The national committee is authorized and empowered to select an Executive Committee from the members of the Republican National Committee, to consist of fifteen (15) members; in addition the following shall serve as ex-officio members of the Executive Committee: The chairman, the co-chairman, the deputy chairman (if any), the vice-chairmen, the secretary, the treasurer, the general counsel, the chairman of the Republican Finance Committee, the president of the National Federation of Republican Women, the chairman of the Republican State Chairmen's Advisory Committee, the chairman of the Young Republican National Federation, the chairman of the College Republican National Committee, the chairman of the National Republican Heritage Groups Council, the chairman of the National Black Republican Council, the chairman of the Republican National Hispanic Assembly, the chairman of the National Conference of Republican Mayors, the Republican leader of the U.S. Senate, the Republican leader of the U.S. House of Representatives, the chairman of the Republican Governors Association, the chairman of the National Conference of Republican County Officials and the chairman of the National Republican Legislators Association.

(b) The Executive Committee may exercise all the executive and administrative functions required of the national committee between meetings of the full committee, with the exception of the following:

(1) election of officers of the national committee,

(2) ratification of members of the Republican National Committee or the Executive Committee,

(3) issuance of the call and designating the time and place for holding the quadrennial national convention,

(4) filling a vacancy in the office of Republican candidate for President or Republican candidate for Vice President.

The Executive Committee shall meet on the call of the chairman, and such meetings shall be held at least once quarterly each year. The minutes of all Executive Committee meetings shall be distributed immediately to all Republican National Committee members.

(c) The chairman, with the approval of the national committee, may appoint other committees and assistants as he or she may deem necessary, and whenever such committees are appointed, they shall consist of a chairman and an equal number of men and womenn.

(d) It shall be the responsibility of the finance chairman to appoint members of a Finance Committee who will be approved in advance by the state chairman of their respective states. The finance chairman, in consultation with the members of the Finance Committee, shall have the duty of developing and implementing a broad-based, fund raising plan.

(e) Upon written petition of at least twenty-five percent (25%) of the members of the Executive Committee, the chairman within ten (10) days shall call a meeting of the Executive Committee to be held in a city to be designated by the chairman. The date of such meeting shall fall between ten (10) and twenty (20) days from the date of the call.

(f) The national committee shall not, without the prior approval of three members of the national committee from the state involved, contribute to any candidate for public or party office except the nominee of the Republican Party or a candidate who is unopposed in the Republican primary after the filing deadline for that office.

RULE No. 27

Vacancies in the national committee shall be ratified by the committee upon the election by the state Republican party in and for the state in which the vacancy occurs. The national committee shall have the power to declare vacant the seat of any member who refuses to support the Republican nominees for President and/or Vice President.

RULE No. 28

(a) The first meeting of the national committee shall take place within fifteen (15) days after the convening of the national convention, upon the call of the member senior in time of service upon the previous national committee; and thereafter upon call of the chairman, or, in case of vacancy in the chairmanship, upon call of the vice chairman senior in time of service on the national committee; but such call shall be issued at least ten (10) days in advance of the date of the proposed meeting. Provided, however, that if one of the purposes of a meeting of the Republican National Committee is to fill a vacancy in the office of Republican candidate for President or Republican candidate for Vice President, then only five (5) days notice of the purpose, date, and place of said meeting shall be required. Upon written petition of sixteen (16) or more members of the national committee, representing not less than sixteen (16) states, filed jointly or separately with the chairman, asking for a meeting of the national committee, it shall be the duty of the chairman within ten (10) days from receipt of said petition to issue a call for a meeting of the national committee, to be held in a city to be designated by the chairman, the date of such called meeting to be not later than twenty (20) days or earlier than ten (10) days from the date of the call.

(b) The Republican National Committee shall meet at least twice a year. A tentative agenda for each meeting shall be mailed to the membership at least ten (10) days prior to the meeting. The minutes, including all resolutions and motions, shall be mailed to all members of the Republican National Committee within thirty (30) days after the close of the meeting.

(c) The annual budget shall be approved at a meeting of the Republican National Committee. The proposed budget, in reasonable detail, shall be mailed to all members of the Republican National Committee at least ten (10) days prior to such meeting.

(d) All meetings of the Republican National Committee and all of its committees shall be open meetings except as provided for by "Robert's Rules of Order Newly Revised."

RULE No. 29

"Robert's Rules of Order Newly Revised" shall govern in all meetings of the national committee insofar as they are applicable and not inconsistent with these rules. At its first meeting, the committee shall make its own rules governing the use of proxies.

Membership in the Next
National Convention

RULE 30

Election of Delegates to
the National Convention

RULE 31

Election of Delegates to
District and State Conventions

RULE 32 through 35

APPENDIX D

Strengthening the Political Parties: A National Position Paper of the Committee on Party Renewal, June 1980

The Committee on Party Renewal is a voluntary group of some two hundred political practitioners and researchers. Bipartisan in membership, we share a common concern for the survival of our political parties. We see them as vital instruments of democracy, but as organizations which are threatened in their very existence.

As we declared at our founding at the Jefferson Memorial in 1977, "Without parties there can be no organized and coherent politics. When politics lacks coherence, there can be no accountable democracy." Without parties, we then warned, we are threatened by "a politics of celebrities, of excessive media influence, of political fad-of-the month clubs, of massive private financing by various 'fatcats' of state and congressional campaigns, of gun-for-hire campaign managers, of heightened interest in 'personalities' and lowered concern for policy, of manipulation and maneuver and management of self-chosen political elites."

As we approach the culmination of the presidential election of 1980, the need for party renewal is even more evident. It has begun to be recognized by respected commentators, by the voting public, and by political leaders of both the Republican and Democratic parties. Discontent with the present arrangements is widespread, as evident in the low degree of trust in our national institutions, in decreased voting turnout, and in the widespread abandonment of party loyalties.

Rebuilding our political parties will require greater involvement by individual citizens, but we are not content to rely on vague urgings of participation.

Effective participation requires appropriate institutional structures, which must be deliberately designed by the parties themselves and by formal statutory change. The actions we recommend are directed toward three goals: increasing the membership of the parties and the effectiveness of political participation; providing the parties with necessary resources, particularly money; and re-establishing functions for the political parties in the overall political system.

Toward these goals, we recommend the following specific actions:

1) Less emphasis should be placed on primary elections for the choice of national convention delegates, while more delegates should be chosen through party caucuses and conventions. Increased representation for party officials is also desirable.

2) If public financing of campaigns is adopted, these funds should be channelled through the parties, with a portion reserved for general party purposes. Direct public financing of the political parties is also widely advocated. Many backers of strengthened parties believe that public funds should be provided for such purposes as party organization, research, publicity, and fund raising, and such support is now provided by a number of states. Other analysts urge increased private support of the parties. While acknowledging these different approaches, we agree that support must be provided to the parties themselves, rather than to individual candidates.

3) The parties should be given more freedom in their financing. Contributions to the parties should be allowed in greater amounts than to individual candidates, and expenditures by parties for research and organization should not be included in campaign expenditure limits. State and local party committees' expenditures on behalf of national slates should not be included in expenditure or contribution limits. In general, party contributions to candidates should be preferred above those of individual or political action committees.

4) State law should provide for party caucuses and conventions, open to all party members, to endorse candidates in the party primary. Such endorsement should be indicated on the primary ballot, with the endorsed candidate normally given the first place on the ballot.

5) Parties should consider holding periodic issue conventions (e.g. in Congressional election years), on the state and national levels. These meetings may invigorate the organization, consider policy questions, and hold officials elected under the party label accountable for the actions on party platform positions.

6) State parties should establish rules that facilitate widespread participation. These rules should include adoption of formal charters, broad public notice of nominating procedures and dates, affirmative action to promote participation by all elements of the population, and apportionment of representation in party bodies on the basis of population and/or electoral strength within the party.

7) Local parties should regularly hold open, well-publicized meetings, at which current issues and contemporary problems are discussed. Positions adopted at such meetings should be forwarded to state and national platform committees.

8) Parties should establish a dues-paying membership. For modest fees, the parties should provide these members with such benefits as copies of the national platform and other policy statements, and a regular report of activities. They should regularly determine members' opinions, and provide information on means to influence the choice of convention delegates and party officials.

9) Federal law should be amended to provide regular access to television for the major political parties. In particular, debates for president and other major offices should be under the control of party bodies, such as the national party committees. Access should also be provided for third-party and independent candidates with sizeable followings.

10) The political parties should establish commissions nationally, and in each state, to promote joint efforts to strengthen the parties, particularly through public education programs and statutory change. Training and research programs through academic institutions should be developed.

(Reprinted from "Party Line," an informal occasional newsletter of the Committee on Party Renewal, Eagleton Institute, Rutgers University.)

Index